SUPERCARS

W9-CEP-388

SUPERCARS

THE WORLD'S BEST SUPERCARS IN 500 GREAT PHOTOS

Graham Robson

This edition first published in 2003 by Crestline, an imprint of
MBI Publishing Company, Galtier Plaza, Suite 200,
380 Jackson Street, St. Paul, MN 55101-3885 USA

MBI Publishing Company books are also available at discounts
in bulk quantity for industrial or sales-promotional use.
For details write to Special Sales Manager at Motorbooks
International Wholesalers & Distributors, Galtier Plaza,
Suite 200, 380 Jackson Street, St. Paul, MN 55101-3885 USA.

ISBN 0-7603-1562-0

Designed and edited by:
FOCUS PUBLISHING, 11a St Botolph's Road, Sevenoaks,
Kent, England TN13 3AJ
Editor: Caroline Watson
Designer: David Etherington

Salamander editor: Marie Clayton

Printed and bound in China

CONTENTS

THE HISTORY OF

SUPERCARS

Next time you are blown off by a blood-red Ferrari, find yourself gazing longingly at a Viper in a showroom, don't get depressed. You're allowed desire, maybe a bit of envy, but don't let it get you. You may admit that you have lusted after a Porsche Turbo for years, but that doesn't make future ownership come any closer. Take heart. Although you have a disease, and it is incurable, you're not about to die. You're in love, for sure—in love with a "Supercar."

Left: Supercars are excitingly-styled, hand-built, and always expensive. This part-completed Lamborghini Countach shows why.

What is a Supercar?

This may be the most difficult job any motoring enthusiast can have. How on earth can I define a "Supercar"? It means different things to different auto enthusiasts. What is a "Supercar" anyway? It's easy enough to point out a Ferrari Boxer, or a Lamborghini Miura—and, somehow, we don't have to think twice? Somehow you just know. But can there be "Supercars" which carry five people in comfort? Must a "Supercar" always be classically beautiful? Can it ever have sold in large numbers?

Maybe the best thing is to fall back on a dictionary definition. According to the famous Oxford English Dictionary, "super" refers to something "higher in status," "to a great or extreme degree," or something "above or beyond or over"....

That's better. Now I'm beginning to understand. I guess we may be getting somewhere. In this colorful world of motor car enthusiasm, to qualify as a "Supercar," a machine has to be really special. But special—how special? Being tire-strippingly fast just isn't good enough. Not on its own. Being beautiful helps, but that isn't enough either. Some of the world's most stunning cars were stately limousines, yet they are certainly not supercars. Being rare won't do the job either: far too many cars were rare because they were commercial failures—they simply didn't sell.

How many different motor cars have been built since the first creaky Daimler and Benz models struggled on to the road in the 1880s? Tens of thousands of models, hundreds of millions of individual cars, for sure—but you wouldn't like to remember many of them as supercars. Most were marketed by businessmen wanting to make a dollar, rather than a reputation.

Most cars were plain rather than pretty, cheap rather than soul stirring—and many were just plain disappointing. Many were soon forgotten—and rightly so. But not the supercars: how many people bought AC Cobras in the 1960s? Only hundreds. But how many of us remember them? All of us. That is what helps to define a supercar.

Right: Every supercar should look dramatic, should have an extrovert character, and when driven should also sound as powerful as it looks. On those counts, the Dodge Viper has everything needed to qualify.

WHERE TO BEGIN ?

In the beginning, the first motor cars struggled to make any sort of reputation. For a time it was still an achievement to complete a journey, so no-one—not even a Wall Street tycoon—worried about performance. Persuaded out of his horse-drawn carriage, he was happy just to complete an auto journey without drama. Image? The only image a pioneering motorist wanted to create was that of a man of means.

It wasn't until the 1900s that cars began to feel faster, and to look fast, too. In Europe it was the original Mercedes, and in North America it was the early Cadillacs that made observers sit up and think. Even so, by the time Henry Ford had launched the Model T in North America, the motor car had stopped being a rich man's toy, and was on its way to being Everyman's transport.

Amazingly, before World War II, there were very few truly fast road cars. Designers still had a lot to learn about

Left: Early cars were not beautiful, and certainly not fast, but in 1900 this Lohner-Porsche was a racing car, with all four wheels driven by individual electric motors. Super for its day? Of course.

engines, and few knew much about aerodynamics. Maybe this explains why 100mph was difficult to breach, and why we were so impressed by the few companies like Bugatti, Duesenberg, Hispano-Suiza, Bentley, and Mercedes-Benz, who all broke through that mythical barrier.

Passing 100mph, and passing it with style and grace, was one thing, but passing 120mph, then 150mph, and more, was going to take real enterprise. Accordingly, I think I am justified in opening our Supercars period immediately after that War. Even while most patriots were exhausted, and in some cases their homes and workplaces lay in ruins, brave men were already thinking ahead.

In the late 1940s, the miracle was that any time and finance was available for supercars to be developed. All such cars, by definition, would be expensive to buy and expensive to run—would there be enough rich people around to buy them? If such cars were previewed, would they ever get into production? Would it be worth the gamble of buying a car which might disappear from the market soon afterwards? With so much devastation, and social deprivation, all around, was it even socially acceptable to buy a car like this?

STARTING OVER

In Europe, where most supercars would be bred, the war had changed everything. In 1945 much of the motor industry was in ruins, and many fine personalities had perished. For the next two years, there would be a big clear up, and it was not until 1947 that the first newly-designed cars appeared.

The people needed wheels, any wheels, so priority went into building cars like the VW Beetle and the Renault 4CV that millions could afford. Where the tooling for 1930s-style sporty cars had survived, it was dug out of store. Accordingly, sports cars like the MG TC made it to the USA, but there was no chance of reviving the big, glossy, glamorous, and exciting Mercedes-Benz 540K, or V12 Hispano-Suiza, models. Alfa Romeo and Bugatti had been bombed, as had Alvis and Lagonda, so ... was there any future for truly fast cars?

Amazingly, there was. Rich people had survived, rich people wanted to enjoy their money, and as ever they wanted to enjoy using fast cars. There might not be too many of them who could afford the very best transport, but the demand was still present.

So, what should go into the new breed of top-grade cars? What was essential? What would satisfy the demand? What, in other words, would be trendy?

Because the war, and its after affects, had swallowed up almost ten years, post-war supercars would need to be a real step forward from those of the 1930s. The imperatives of war, however, had already found ways for that to happen. Looking forward to the 1950s, the new breed would need to have more advanced engines, better chassis and—above all—more streamlined looks. Right away 120mph, if not 130mph, would have to be the target top speed—and more would be expected in the next ten years or so.

Late-1930s supercars, after all, had often achieved their reputations without finesse. To produce their performance, engines were usually large and heavy,

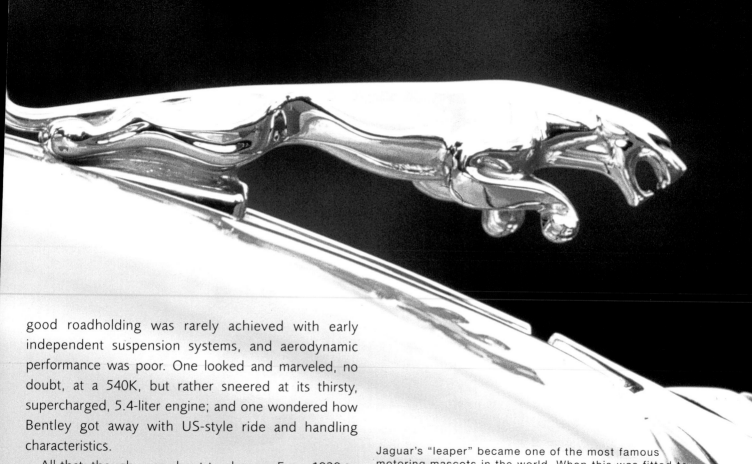

good roadholding was rarely achieved with early independent suspension systems, and aerodynamic performance was poor. One looked and marveled, no doubt, at a 540K, but rather sneered at its thirsty, supercharged, 5.4-liter engine; and one wondered how Bentley got away with US-style ride and handling characteristics.

All that, though, was about to change. From 1939 to 1945, not only had aircraft engines learned to be more

Jaguar's "leaper" became one of the most famous motoring mascots in the world. When this was fitted to the nose, an extra badge was not needed. It was only safety legislation which killed it off in more recent years.

powerful, and to be relatively light, but high-octane fuel had evolved to serve them. Aerodynamicists, too, had learned much about the way to shape machinery, and to cheat the air. In ten years the top speed of fighter aircraft had doubled—from 300mph to 600mph—and bright engineers now knew how to apply such advances to motor cars.

Even before the world's fastest cars were re-positioned, therefore, the pundits were agreed on what they should contain: they would need to have forward-looking, and softly-streamlined bodywork; they would need to have more advanced and more efficient engines; and they would need to have the most advanced chassis yet seen.

In the 1920s, the big leap forward had been in engine layouts (side valve to overhead valve), and in the 1930s it head been in chassis layouts (independent front suspension and box-section frames). Now, in the 1940s, two parallel leaps were forecast.

Left: The Mercedes-Benz 540K was one of the world's fastest supercars in the 1930s, exceeding 100mph, but there was no place for such a heavy monster in the late 1940s.

One was in the nature of body styles, which would not only look sinuous but would push their way more easily through the air, the other in the layout and performance of engines, where one or even two overhead camshafts would be expected.

It was an exciting time to wait for the new cars—and that wait was well worth the suspense. Amazingly, the arrival of the first two contenders was quite unexpected, for neither of them had featured in the 1930s.

The first post-war car which really stirred the blood came from Italy. Alfa Romeo might still be in ruins, but the man who had once ran their racing teams was not. In 1948 a brand-new company called Ferrari delivered its very first Type 166, from a factory at Maranello, and it was immediately clear that something out of the ordinary was taking place. Only months later, from Coventry, the British city whose heart had been flattened by the Luftwaffe in 1940, came Jaguar's astonishing XK120. In both cases, the sensation came in their engines. One, the Ferrari, was expensive, while the Jaguar started at an amazingly low selling price. These were pointers to the future—for Ferraris would always be exclusive, and sell in hundreds, while Jaguars (although no less adventurous, technically), would sell in tens of thousands.

Although the Ferrari contented itself with single overhead camshaft valve gear, this was in an all-new and compact vee-12 layout. Not the world's first vee-12 road

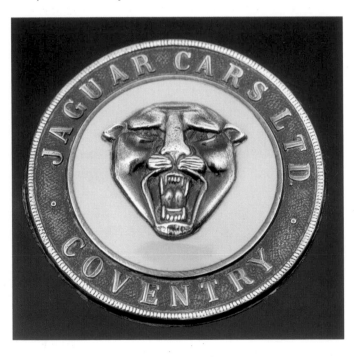

car engine by any means—Cadillac, Lincoln, Rolls-Royce, Lagonda, and Hispano-Suiza all got there in the 1930s, for instance—but definitely the most advanced so far.

Although the early examples only produced 110bhp from 2-liter engines, the Ferrari's potential was never in doubt. On the day that Ferrari was born, so was Ferrari mania, and many of today's enthusiasts can still recite how that engine would grow, and grow, and grow—to well over 3 liters, and well over 350bhp. There have been other types of Ferrari engine, some with a lot more power —but that classic vee-12 remains to this day.

Jaguar, on the other hand, chose a more classic layout —a straight-six with a twin-overhead camshaft layout. Nothing exciting there, you might say, for there had been racing engines of this type since the 1920s. But here was the difference—the XK engine was to be the world's first twin-cam engine to go into series-production (there were very few pre-war Alfas and Duesenbergs, after all), and

Left: Every Supercar manufacturer developed his own individual style, including the way the cars were identified. This was the legendary Jaguar symbol of the post-war period.

to go into sports cars and saloons alike. With 160bhp from 3.4-liters, it was a big leap ahead of anything which the British motor industry had offered in the 1930s.

Both cars had independent suspension, though it was the Jaguar which showed most enterprise. The Italian car's system used a transverse leaf spring which put pragmatism ahead of mechanical elegance, while that of the Jaguar used longitudinal torsion bars, in a layout which must surely have been influenced by the front-wheel-drive Citroën of the 1930s. Ferrari would dump the leaf spring in the 1950s, though Jaguar's neat torsion bar system would be used all the way into the 1970s.

Right: Jaguar's XK120 changed the face of supercar motoring in the 1940s, with a sleek new style, an ultra-modern twin-cam engine, and a top speed of 125mph which set new standards. Few pre-war cars could even reach 100mph.

For their styling, both cars embraced the same basic themes. Both had full-width body treatment, with swooping lines. Running boards, which had been everywhere in the 1930s, had completely disappeared, and headlamps were faired neatly into the bodywork. Interestingly, although the Jaguar looked more sexy, it retained some semblance of

Above: Ferrari! What a legendary name this would become. The first vee-12 engined cars were delivered in 1947 and, fifty years later, the legend lives on.

wing lines, while the more conventional Ferraris at least featured a smooth barchetta shape.

The Ferrari, maybe, was not as fast as it looked, but all the potential for future growth was obviously present, while the noise of that magnificent new vee-12 engine, and the sheer flamboyant character of the ensemble, stirred the blood. Even so, with up to 120mph already available, this neat little two-seater already laid down a marker.

The Jaguar, however, was different in so many ways, Sexy to look at, comfortable to drive in, and amazingly flexible in traffic, it proved that twin-cam engines did not have to be temperamental. And it was quick, too. Closed-road tests of a near standard two-seater showed that 132mph was possible—even if 125mph was more usual for an off-the-line example—and that 100mph+ cruising was easily within every owner's reach.

Both these cars, of course, were already much faster than the elite of the 1930s. A Mercedes-Benz 540K could perhaps reach an honest 105mph, as could a Type 57

Bugatti, but in those days anything faster had been well out of reach. So, if a 20 per cent advance had been achieved at the first attempt, what more might be seen in the 1960s, and beyond? Was 150mph feasible? Was, whisper it softly, even 200mph attainable? Since the phrase "politically incorrect" had not even been invented, no-one was about to say that such speeds were anti-social, and the world of car enthusiasms waited impatiently to find out.

Below: Early Ferraris were unashamedly based on racing sports car engineering. This Touring-styled 166 Inter was available either as a "Barchetta" roadster, or a closed coupe.

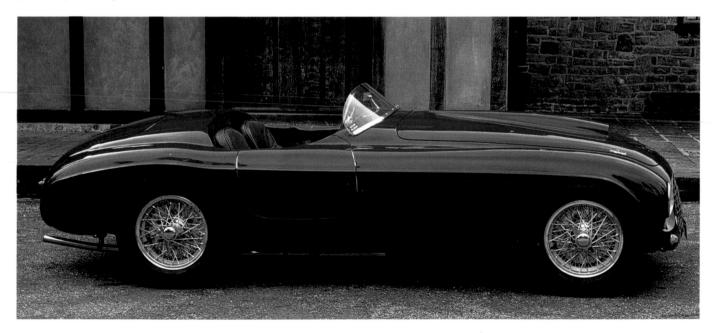

NEW CHASSIS LAYOUTS

In the next few years, it took an age for the would-be supercar manufacturers to join in the hunt for prestige sales. Maserati already made road cars—but not very many, and not very fast—Aston Martin decided to work up slowly from a slower (but more expensive) base, while Bentley originally preferred to make hundreds of excellent saloons, rather than dozens of fine coupes.

Although Ferrari continued to head all the lists—if not in numbers built, but in the sheer variety of vee-12-engined road cars on offer—it was Mercedes-Benz, with the 300SL, who provided the real novelty. After spending years rebuilding a shattered business (the USAF and the RAF· had comprehensively flattened the German factories in 1944 and 1945), they finally got back into motor racing. It was the 300SL, first conceived as a racing sports car, which finally went on general sale.

At a stroke, the 300SL made all previous supercars look antique. Not only was this a car which would reach 150mph if the gearing was right (just a few large-engined

Ferraris would do the same, later in the decade), but it contained so much novelty.

Having been away for so long, Mercedes-Benz embraced every possible advance to make their point, drawing on aircraft engineering knowledge to help them. Not only did they produce the world's first direct fuel-injected automotive petrol engine, but they wrapped it in a complex multi-tube space-frame chassis. Not only did they provide all-independent suspension, but they clothed the whole in a style where the coupe doors opened upwards, rather than swung out in the normal way.

Customers soon found out that the 300SL's handling wasn't up to much, but there were never any doubts about the performance—or the sheer sex appeal—of this amazingly-styled coupe. If it was Ferrari which set the

Left: Test equipment was often still simple in the 1950s. Much of the enterprise, and technical bravery, was safely stored in the engineers' hearts.

Below: By any standards, the Mercedes-Benz 300SL of 1954 was the most advanced supercar of the decade. Not only were the lift-up "gullwing" doors unique, but there was a multi-tube chassis, and a fuel-injected engine.

post-war tone, it was the 300SL which emphasized the excesses which were to follow. Later in the decade, with a conventional convertible body style, and more capable rear suspension, the 300SL was at once more saleable, but less special.

Although Ferrari could never match this tour de force with similar engineering, it made up for everything with a series of bigger, ever more powerful, and brutally fast machines, all of them with individually styled bodies, and all of them with that deliciously melodious type of vee-12 engines.

Or, rather, two types of vee-12 engines. By the time the 342 America and 410 Superamerica models had arrived in the mid-1950s, they were based around a new and more massive vee-12, the 410 being a 340bhp/5.0-liter power unit which ensured a staggering 165mph. With performance like that, it really didn't matter that Ferrari build quality was poor, and that Enzo Ferrari himself admitted

Left: Ferrari believed in testing everything to the limit before making it available for sale, often using the race track as their testing ground.

that road cars were only needed to make profits for him to go motor racing.

With the DB4, and especially the DB4GT, both of which had Italian styling, Aston Martin finally made cars which were equal to the Ferrari in all but image, while BMW (also, like Mercedes-Benz, back from war-time devastation), made a few open-top 507s. The most intriguing, but short-lived, newcomer was the Spanish Pegaso Z102. Because its designer was Wilfredo Ricart (one time technical chief at Alfa Romeo), Pegaso operated from a one-time Hispano-Suiza factory, and the engine was a twin-cam vee-8, it had all the best DNA. However, the Spaniards, somehow, were never truly committed to building up the name, and the project was dropped after only seven years.

Fame in the 1950s, therefore, was shared between Ferrari and Mercedes-Benz, but all that was about to change. Exciting new names, and famous new marques, were waiting in the wings.

Left: At Ferrari, the same team of engineers worked on engines for road cars, or for race cars like these Type 625 single-seaters of 1953.

EARLY MID-ENGINED SUPERCARS

There were enormous changes and advances in supercar production during the 1960s. Not only did the first mid-engined supercars appear (the Lamborghini Miuras and the Ferrari Dino among them), but there were fascinating new ranges from Iso, Lamborghini, and Maserati. Aston Martin and Jaguar both improved on their previous best, while Detroit finally got in on the act by supplying power for cars as diverse as the AC Cobra, the de Tomaso Mangusta, and the Iso Grifo.

Two cars changed the face of supercars—forever. One was the sleek and sexy Jaguar E-Type, while the other was the Lamborghini Miura. Nothing that Ferrari could do — and it tried so hard, especially with the Daytona and the 365 California—could match the enterprise of those rivals.

The Miura was special, not only because it had a mid/rear-engined layout, but also because the massive vee-12 engine was actually mounted across the chassis, and because the style was simply mouthwatering. So, what if the nose tended to lift when it neared its 170mph top speed! The clientele didn't seem to mind…

Left: Ferruccio Lamborghini adopted this emblem, showing a fighting bull, as the symbol of his new company's strength.

Right: Jaguar's E-Type was the world's first supercar to have its style evolved in a wind-tunnel. This was a 4.2-liter model from 1965.

The E-Type was special because its prices were always so ridiculously low. No-one had previously seen something quite so obviously shaped with the wind in mind, and no-one could see how Jaguar could possibly sell a 150mph car at such prices. The fact that the coupe was an eminently practical fastback/hatchback made up for everything, even a tendency for it to overheat in a Californian rush hour. Before long, more than 100

Left: Ferrari's new "small" car—badged Dino—was its first mid-engined road-car.

Right: Supercars have always been assembled by hand, and by craftsmen.

E-Types were being built (and sold) every week—at a time when Ferrari was still used to selling such quantities of a model every year.

In other words, the supercar benchmarks had been notched up considerably. If 130mph had been a good qualifying achievement in the 1940s, and 150mph in the 1950s, suddenly 170mph was needed in the 1960s. By no means every supercar achieved such figures, but many left 150mph far behind. Gas was still cheap and plentiful, the post-war economic boom was generating more and more millionaires to enjoy their wealth, and now there were at least six makers ready to supply them.

Ferrari, need I emphasize, were still market leaders, if not trendsetters. As model after model—250GT Lusso, 275GTB, and 365GTB/4 Daytona—followed, and as the smaller mid-engined Dino 206/246 range matured, they were all real icons. However, in the 1960s they had to face up to real competition—local competition, no less—from Maserati, Lamborghini, and Iso. Additionally, from the UK came Aston Martins, which were better, faster, and equally as attractive—and there were more of them.

But with the 1970s looming, and with more mid-engined supercars on the way, was the balance of power about to change ?

REACHING FOR 170MPH

In the 1970s, it was a miracle that supercars survived at all. First there was the Yom Kippur war of 1973, which led to the Energy Crisis, the hike in oil prices, and the world-wide cost inflation which followed. Then in 1979 the Shah (of Iran) left town, and the Second Energy Crisis followed. To crown all, politicians' moods were swinging against indulgence, and against excess...

Amazingly, many excellent new cars kept on coming, for there were still enough well-heeled people who wanted to spit defiance at the world, and its increasingly politically-correct tendencies. One way to do this was for them to spend the price of a small house on a glossy, sinuous-looking, car which usually cost a fortune to maintain—but which told us everything about the owner's character.

Although the ultimate top speed requirement had not notched up again—170mph was still quite enough, for the time being—new cars got bigger, heavier, and more powerful. Even so, it was interesting to see that practical supercars—some of them with two seats, and all of them with front-mounted engines—often found more customers than their self-indulgent mid/rear-engined, two-seater relatives.

Need I emphasize that while three Italian marques—Ferrari, Lamborghini, and Maserati—made most of the headlines, it was Porsche which moved the goalposts. In the 1960s the rear-engined 911 had been a good car, if not a great product, but from 1975 it was turbocharged and became sensational. If you were a good driver (and this helped, especially with all that weight around the tail), the 300bhp 911 Turbo could whip any of its rivals—and all allied to German build quality, and detail attention to engineering.

Worldwide, it seemed, the "engine-behind-cabin" layout was now the norm. Not only did Ferrari produce the monstrously powerful flat-12 engined Boxer, but the smaller, yet very saleable, 308GTB. Lamborghini added

Below: Porsche's supercar layout of the 1970s—with a turbocharged, air-cooled flat-six engine mounted in the tail—was unique. This attractive car outsold all its rivals.

the smaller Urraco (not a success), and the sharply-styled Countach (another trendsetter, especially in its style), while Maserati produced the simpler, but still effective, Bora and Merak types. Even Lotus of England, with small turbocharged four-cylinder power, produced the exciting Esprit Turbo—which James Bond soon made famous in movies. Amazingly, the Aston Martin Vantage was one of the fastest of all.

There were casualties, though, in the market place. Iso of Milan ran out of money—which therefore denied the supercar market to Chevrolet—Aston Martin engineering stagnated (they were short of money, too), while Jaguar finally jettisoned the E-Type in favor of a much larger, definitely non-supercar, the XJ-S.

All in all, this was not a decade to encourage newcomers, either. Even so, Lancia was encouraged to introduce the tiny, wedge-snouted Stratos, which made up for a relatively small engine (Ferrari vee-6), with huge quantities of charisma and Latin-style machismo; it was a great rally car, too.

Right: The lines of this artist's rendering have been simplified, but the appeal of a mid-engined Ferrari is immediately obvious.

4WD, 200MPH—AND MORE

After the traumas of the 1970s, there was something of a lull in the supercar stakes, before the effects of the "Greed is Good" period began to take hold again. The developed world shrugged off the second Energy Crisis, inflation subsided, and worldwide prosperity returned once again. By the end of the 1980s the first of the near-200mph road cars began to appear.

This was also the period in which the so-called "classic" value of older supercars went through the roof. In the 1970s some two-seater projectiles had gone right out of fashion, but as entrepreneurs became rich once more, they began to buy more toys—Big Boys' Toys. Until the very cusp of the 1990s, many believed that classic car values were going to rise indefinitely, and that there was money to be made. That was a big mistake, as the worldwide recession of the early 1990s would prove.

More than previously, this was the decade when new supercars could not only boast huge performance, but new technology as well. For the very first time, Chevrolet introduced a Corvette which qualified—the ZR1,

Above: Enzo Ferrari (center) ran his own car company for more than 40 years.

Right: In the mid-1980s, Porsche's 959 was a triumph of technology.

complete with its Lotus-developed twin-cam, vee-8 engine—while even Ford-of-Europe produced the shapely, Ghia-styled four-wheel-drive RS200—a rally car tamed for road use, but none-the-less attractive for all that.

Nothing, however, could beat Porsche's magnificent, and painstakingly-developed 959 model—a four-wheel-drive, twin-turbocharged masterpiece which was once

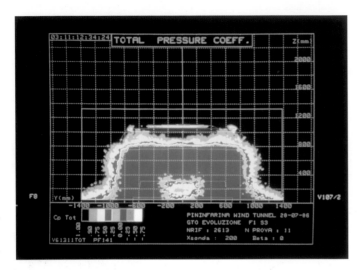

the world had yet seen—the flat-12 engined Testarossa, the turbocharged vee-8-powered 288GTO, and finally the 200mph F40, which was a fortieth-birthday present to the company and all its faithful customers.

Although Porsche's engineering was supreme, only Ferrari could offer such a spine-tingling blend of all the latest supercar virtues. Lamborghini hit so many financial problems that they gave up trying for years, BMW's M1

Above: Wind-tunnel testing had become very scientific by the 1980s.

Right: Ferrari Testarossa assembly under way at Maranello in the late 1980s.

aimed at Group B motorsport, but ended up as the ultimate high-performance road car for those who appreciated all-corners-covered German development expertise.

Ferrari, no doubt, felt uncomfortable about this, but they didn't let it show. Instead they produced three of the most drop-dead-gorgeous mid/rear-engined two-seaters was a strange mix of German engine expertise and small-town Italian build quality, while the latest French MVS and Alpine-Renault types relied on lightweight construction to deliver their performance.

Although Ferrari virtually abandoned front-engined cars in the 1980s (but they would be back...), they seemed to cover almost all the bases, from the "small" 328s and 348tbs, to the 5-liter Testarossas. Other companies copied them—sometimes in their layout, sometimes in a study of their mechanical components—but none could emulate their legendary reputation. The fact that they had been backed by truckloads of Fiat finance since 1969 made this doubly hard to bear.

Below: Supercars like the Ferrari F40 were so fast that extensive wind-tunnel testing was needed to make them stable at high road speeds.

NAME NAMES, NEW TARGETS

In the first few years of the 1990s, some of the world's most extraordinary supercars finally appeared. Conceived in the late 1980s, when motoring prospects seemed limitless, they often failed commercially in the recession-hit 1990s—but their technical reputation will live on.

The 200mph barrier was not only breached, but brushed ruthlessly aside. Jaguar's XJ220 could certainly approach 220mph (that was the reason for its model name, after all...), and there were signs that the Bugatti EB110 and the Cizeta-Moroder V16T might do the same. This, though, was all made obsolete when McLaren's F1 road car, complete with 6-liter BMW power, was officially timed at 231mph. Game, set, and match—and even ten years on that figure had never officially been beaten.

The variety of cars was amazing. Apart from McLaren, Bugatti, and Cizeta-Moroder, there were other mid-rear engined supercars from Ferrari (512TR/512M), Honda NSX, Jaguar XJ220, Lamborghini Diablo, Mercedes-Benz CLK-GTR, and several Porsche 911 derivatives. TVR chimed in with the thunderous front-engined Griffith,

Cerbera, and Chimaera types, while Aston Martin launched the excellent DB7 family.

Not only that, but the Dodge Viper ("son of Cobra," if only in spirit) made a real impact in its native USA, while Ferrari's first gift to Maserati (which it had absorbed) was the launch of the 3200GT—easily the best car to grace that badge for twenty years.

The entire supercar industry seemed to have concluded that it could reach the extremes of every performance envelope, push the barriers out even farther, and produce miraculously beautiful, fast, and capable machinery. No longer did a supercar have to trade off refinement or reliability in the quest for tire-stripping performance. Engine and aerodynamic technology had now advanced so far that the only limits appeared to be cost, and public opinion.

In 1992 a car like the latest (front-engined) Ferrari 550 Maranello could not only carry more than two passengers in air-conditioned comfort, but it was both quiet and flexible

Left: TVR joined the supercar league with this Cerbera in the 1990s—not only with its own individual front-engined style, but with its own unique vee-8 engine, also.

around town. Automatic transmission eventually became optional (and, yes, there was a market for this), electronically adjustable damping was all part of the package—yet this was in a 442bhp/5.5-liter vee-12-engined chassis that could break any speed limit, in any condition, anywhere.

It was good to see new names, too—successfully from Honda, whose aluminum-hulled NSX was the first supercar ever to come from Japan, and from Bentley (now owned by Audi-VW), who showed the Hunaudières project car just to demonstrate that they eventually intended to change the face of cars to be built behind the Flying B.

Though the economic downturn hit the Supermarket in the mid-1990s, there was real cause for celebration at the end of the century. Famous names still survived, while others, such as Aston Martin, Bentley, Lamborghini, and Maserati were cosily protected by larger concerns. Was there more to come in the new century?

Below: The aluminum-shelled, mid-engined Honda NSX was the first supercar to be developed in Japan.

250MPH NEXT?

There was, and joyfully so. Vibrant new machinery appeared from unexpected corners—Mosler, Panoz, and Saleen from the USA, Pagani from Italy, and Noble from Great Britain—while Ford-USA elected to bring the legendary old GT40 back to life, and even Cadillac produced the Cien project car, which sadly remained a one-off.

Although the traditional supercar pecking order was undisturbed—Ferrari, as ever, was top of the heap, Porsche was close behind, while Maserati was well-and-truly reborn—it was the newcomers which caused so much excitement in the new century.

Helped along by Ford-USA finance, and by Cosworth's sorcery in developing a vee-12 engine, Aston Martin produced the magnificent 450bhp front-engined Vanquish, while VW poured money into the historic old Bentley factory and prepared to launch the technologically superb vee-12 engined, four-wheel-drive Continental Coupe.

The march of technology, also, was impressive. Carbon fiber had been a space age material in the 1970s, which fed

Above: What's in a badge? Everything. The winged-B denotes a Bentley, as it was, as it is today, and for the future under VW.

across to race cars in the 1980s, but by 2000 it found normal usage in road cars. Ex-F1 "paddle" gearchange levers found a regular home behind steering wheels, semi-automatic transmissions became usual, and everything from engine management to suspension settings came to be controlled electronically. Air conditioning, anti-lock braking, ride-height adjustment, and the automatic deployment of spoilers were all taken for granted.

It was an exciting time to have the money, and the interest, in motoring far and fast, for several far-flung companies now seemed to have discovered ways of building such cars profitably, too. And there was more to come in 2004 and beyond. Not only was McLaren of

England preparing to build the new Mercedes-Benz SLR, but Bugatti (another marque now nestling in the Audi-VW stable) was ready to launch the 1,000bhp Veyron model. Not only was Ferrari's uncontested position— not only as a traditional maker of supercars, but as the most prestigious, also—finally in doubt, but top speeds of more than 250mph could now be forecast with confidence.

So, we now live in a politically-correct world, right? Maybe—but that doesn't stop the world's car-makers hatching plans to produce more, better, faster, and simply mind-boggling supercars in the future.

Right: A vee-12 engined Vanquish coupe during assembly at the Aston Martin factory in England. Financial backing by Ford, engine by Cosworth, but character and spirit definitely by Aston Martin, of course.

CHAPTER 1

1950s

Two marques dominated the decade, for different reasons. Ferrari somehow produced a flood of different vee-12 engined models, all on the same type of tubular chassis, but with many different styles. Mercedes-Benz, on the other hand, made all other supercars obsolete with its advanced 300SL, gullwing doors, space frame chassis, and all. The benchmark top speed became 150mph, which some of the largest Ferrari could beat with ease.

The Mercedes-Benz 300SL made all other supercars look old-fashioned. There was a space-frame chassis, all-independent suspension, a fuel-injected engine hidden away—and the doors opened upwards.

Left: In 1952
Bentley's R-Type
Continental
brought supercar
motoring into the
realms of the
carriage trade.
This full four-
seater coupe
was the fastest
Bentley so far
put on sale.

Right: Only 22
of Ferrari's 340
America model
were ever made.
Built in 1951–2,
all of them
featured a
22bhp/4.1-liter
vee-12 engine,
the first to use
the big
"Lampredi" vee-
12 power unit.

FERRARI 166

Ferrari's first racing sports car was the Type 125, and this car, the 2-liter/Type 166 Inter, followed it from 1948 to 1951. The heart of this machine was Colombo's amazing vee-12, which would eventually grow to 3.3-liters in the 1960s, and it ran in a chassis with tubular members and reinforcements. Ferrari never

Above: The 2-liter 166 Inter engine was the first road-going example of Ferrari's legendary new vee-12 engine, and was fitted with Weber carburation.

Above: The 166 Inter's rev counter was calibrated all the way to 8,000rpm, for the 2-liter vee-12 was a very free-revving engine.

built its own bodies, so coupe and cabriolet styles were provided by specialists such as Touring, Allemano, Ghia, Vignale, and Stabilimenti Farina. This was merely the start of a glittering career for the Italian marque.

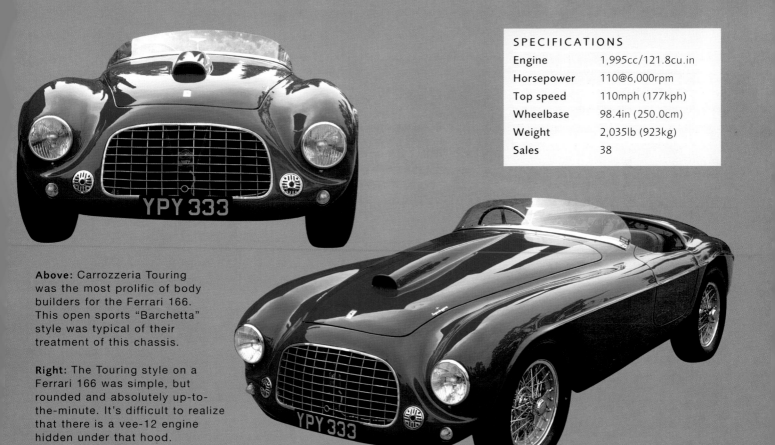

SPECIFICATIONS

Engine	1,995cc/121.8cu.in
Horsepower	110@6,000rpm
Top speed	110mph (177kph)
Wheelbase	98.4in (250.0cm)
Weight	2,035lb (923kg)
Sales	38

Above: Carrozzeria Touring was the most prolific of body builders for the Ferrari 166. This open sports "Barchetta" style was typical of their treatment of this chassis.

Right: The Touring style on a Ferrari 166 was simple, but rounded and absolutely up-to-the-minute. It's difficult to realize that there is a vee-12 engine hidden under that hood.

Left: Until the mid-1950s, Ferrari styling was restrained, and all the cars were two-seaters.

Below: On early Ferraris, there was always a comprehensive display of instruments.

JAGUAR XK120

Though launched in 1948, Jaguar's XK120 came to maturity early in the 1950s, when Roadster, fixed-head, and drop-head-coupe versions all became available. It was 30mph faster than any previous Jaguar, and was powered by the wonderful six-cylinder XK engine, which would be Jaguar's mainstay for the next thirty years.

Above: The XK120 had a tiny grille—the engine sometimes overheated.

Above: Launched as a 160bhp/3.4-liter engine, the XK always looked impressive, and powerful.

Left: The XK120 was personally styled by Jaguar's founder, William Lyons.

The XK140 grew old gracefully, becoming the XK140 in 1954 (with more power and a larger cabin), and finally the XK150 in 1957, with a restyled body. Each and every version was refined, incredibly flexible to drive, and sold for astonishingly little money.

Right: Fixed-head coupe versions of the XK120 sports car had a handsome walnut veneer dashboard.

SPECIFICATIONS

Engine	3,442cc/210cu.in
Horsepower	160@5,000rpm
Top speed	125mph (210kph)
Wheelbase	102in (259cm)
Weight	2,910lb (1,320kg)
Sales	12,078

Far left: Jaguar's XK120 offered a startling combination of good lucks, high performance, modern engineering, and value for money. It was an instant success.

Left: The Bentley S-Type Continental appeared in 1955, on the new S-class chasssis, and was available in several four-seater coachbuilt styles, open or closed.

Above: Bentley also made full five-seater four-door Continentals in the 1950s, these carrying the name of "Flying Spur," and produced by H.J.Mulliner in significant numbers.

Left: By the mid-1950s, Ferrari vee-12s had been expanded to 3-liters. This Pininfarina-styled coupe was one of several different coupes offered on the same vee-12 theme at the time. All of them could beat 130mph, and all of them were very desirable.

Right: A 3-liter vee-12 engined Ferrari of course, and a Pininfarina body, of course, but there were many variations on the same styling theme in the mid-1950s. This is a 250 Europa. Several other such Ferraris had almost the same nose, oval grille, and extra-driving-lamp treatment.

Above: Jaguar was proud of its race record at Le Mans, and on the XK140 it made sure that those successes were recorded in the badge carried on the trunk lid.

Left: When the Jaguar XK120 became the XK140 in 1954, the front grille was altered, to have fewer, wider-spaced bars, to allow more cooling air into the radiator.

Right: Although based on the same chassis as the XK120, the XK140 was different in many ways. Not only was there a different front grille and full-size fenders, but there was rack-and-pinion steering for the first time.

Left: There were three versions of the XK140, this being the fixed-head coupe.

Right: The XK140 was a more substantially built car than the XK120 which it replaced in 1954. Traffic conditions demanded more solid fenders and a better-breathing radiator.

Below: Although the XK140 always carried this badge in its front grille, the shape was so recognizable that it would not have needed any more identification.

Below: Facel Vega was a new French marque in the 1950s, from a company which had previously built body shells for others. Original cars like this FV Cabriolet were powered by Chrysler V8 engines.

Right: Small styling cues on this Facel Vega FV Cabriolet, denoting the first true French supercar for some years.

Above: Facel Vega of Paris—a proud new badge in the 1950s, but one which would only exist for another decade.

Right: Facel Vega's boss, Jean Daninos, had his own ideas about styling—the original FV-type of the mid-1950s being an evolution of those shells he had already shaped for other French manufacturers.

Left: By launching the DB4 in 1958, Aston Martin moved up into the realms of supercar manufacture, as this was a 3.7-liter twin-cam engined machine which carried up to four people, could reach 140mph, and had a stunning body style which had been prepared by Carrozzeria Touring of Italy.

Right: In 1958 the new Aston Martin DB4 was a handsome grand-touring supercar, totally different from its smaller-engined predecessors. Cars of this family would be developed, and improved, over the next 12 years.

MERCEDES-BENZ 300SL

Although Mercedes-Benz took years to recover from the devastation and damage of World War II, the wait was worthwhile. First built for racing in 1952 then (urged on by their North American distributor), for sale as a road car in 1954, the sensational 300SL was developed by the German firm.

Although the engine, gearbox, rear axle, and some suspension components were all evolved from those of the modern 300 saloon, there was a brand-new multi-tube space frame chassis, a remarkable body style in which the doors opened upwards (rather than outwards), and the engine itself was treated to direct fuel injection, fifty years before it become normal on any other automotive petrol engine.

The frame of the Mercedes 300SL had been inspired by aeronautical engineering, but because of the depth of the sill members the

Above: The instrument display was comprehensive, but the driving position was a little cramped.

Left: Not much stowage space in the trunk of a 300SL, due to the big spare wheel.

Right: Mercedes-Benz adopted "gullwing door" openings for the 300SL because the sills were very high, and conventional doors could not be fitted.

Left: The 300SL was an all-new style from Mercedes-Benz, with features that included cooling grilles to help get hot air out of the engine bay, eyebrows over the front and rear wheelarches, and center-lock wheels as optional extras.

door operation was purely practical. With no less than 240bhp and a good aerodynamic shape, here was a car that could exceed 150mph with appropriate gearing, though originally its swing-axle rear suspension made it difficult to drive fast .

From 1957 Mercedes-Benx changed the frame and made the 300SL into a Roadster, with conventional doors. Disc brakes were also added before production ended in 1963.

Above: The speedometer on the 300SL was calibrated up to as much as 160mph.

Left: The facia and instrument display of the original 300SL.

Right: The 300SL's shape was smooth and carefully-contoured.

Left: Entry and exit from the 300SL's driving seat would not have been easy.

Right: The famous three-pointed star of Mercedes-Benz.

Below: The 300SL's style was flamboyant, but also practical.

Left: Ferrari's SuperAmerica series of vee-12 engined cars were the biggest, the best, and the fastest of all such front-engined cars. The instruments of this 400 model tell their own story.

Below: The style of Ferrari SuperAmerica types evolved rapidly during the late 1950s and early 1960s. This Pininfarina style dates from the early 1960s, when the design was at its height.

Right: This Pininfarina-styled Ferrari 400 SuperAmerica was one of several shapes seen on this massively powerful chassis, and though looking large, it was strictly a two-seater.

Left: Aston Martin's DB5 was always a great car, but became world famous for its use in the James Bond film *Goldfinger*. The styling was by Carrozzeria Touring.

Below: The DB5 had a 282bhp/4.0-liter six-cylinder twin-cam engine and could reach more than 140mph. This was Aston Martin's most popular model of the 1960s.

Left: BMW's new two-seater 507 was developed with North American sales in mind, and had a 3.2-liter vee-8 engine. With a top speed of nearly 125mph, it was a big and brawny car, which had to compete for sales against the 300SL and the latest Ferraris.

Right: Styled by Count Albrecht Goertz, and inspired by BMW's north American importer Max Hoffman, the two-seater 507 was a complete break from other existing BMW styles of the day. If it had been lighter, and more nimble, the 507 would surely have been a success.

Left: Like every other BMW of that, and later, periods, the 507 could be identified by the famous BMW "spinner" badge on its nose.

Above: The BMW 507 was originally built as a two-seater roadster, but it was also available with this delightfully subtle hardtop.

Right: Ferrari's famous 3-liter vee-12 engined 250GT California model was one of several open-top Ferraris designed for sale in North America.

Left: The Ferrari 250GT California was a wonderful two-seater, of which more than 100 cars were produced from 1958 to 1962. With 250bhp (280bhp on later models), this car represented pure indulgence for a rich owner—and everyone loved them.

Far left: The 250GT California's headlamps were hidden behind clear fairings, to help provide the nose with a better aerodynamic shape. Did this inspire Jaguar to do the same thing?

Left: So typical of all Ferrari interiors of the 1950s period, the 250GT California featured an alloy-spoked, wooden-rimmed steering wheel, with its main instruments ahead of the driver's eyes, and a row of auxiliary controls to impress the passenger.

Right: By the late 1950s, Pininfarina's Ferrari theme was settling down, and a whole list of cues would be carried forward from one model to the next. The oval grille, the faired-in headlamps, and the fresh-air scoop in the hood would all find a use in later models.

FERRARI 250GT SPYDER CALIFORNIA

The Ferrari 250GT Spyder California model was inspired by that arch-enthusiast, Luigi Chinetti, who wanted a specific model to sell in the balmy climes of North America's West Coast. Ferrari indulged him by providing a powerful version of the well-proven 3-liter vee-12-engined chassis,

Right: A Ferrari like this Spyder California is just asking to be driven. Preferably fast, in a warm climate, with the top down...

Left: Real horsepower in a Ferrari Spyder California—250bhp from 3-liters on earlier cars, no less than 280bhp on final models.

and Pininfarina produced a smart two-seater which actually bore some tiny resemblance to the Alfa Romeo Giulietta Spyder from the same styling house. Originally on a longer wheelbase, and finally on a 7.8in- shorter frame with 30bhp extra, the California was built in batches from 1958 to 1962.

SPECIFICATIONS

Engine	2,953cc/180.3cu.in
Horsepower	250@7,000rpm
Top speed	150mph (241kph)
Wheelbase	102.4in (260.0cm)
Weight	2,370lb (1,075kg)
Sales	47 LWB; 57 SWB

Very few people could afford a 250GT Spyder California. What a treat to own one!

In spite of its size, and price, the Spyder California was only a two-seater.

Above: The fuel filler cap of the Zagato-bodied DB4GT was neatly recessed in the rear wing.

Right: Zagato's facia/instrument layout in the Aston Martin DB4GT Zagato was stark and purposeful.

Left: Although Zagato styled the entire body of the Aston Martin DB4GT Zagato, they managed to keep a "family face," which made the car instantly recognizable.

Below: Aston Martin's DB4GT was already a smaller and more powerful version of the DB4, but the Zagato-bodied derivative was even more compact. All the body panels were in thin light alloy, and protection from those fenders was really non-existent.

Right: The Spanish Pegaso Z102, of the early 1950s, was one of the rarest of all supercars. Almost every car had individual styling features—on this car there was an engine bay air scoop above the main radiator inlet.

Left: The vee-8 engined Pegaso Z102 was handsome from any angle. If only the Spaniards had been serious about this project, Ferrari might have had to fight hard.

Right: The Pegaso Z102 was only an indulgence by the Spanish state-controlled concern, though its pedigree, through engineer Wilfredo Ricart, was world-class.

Below: Only 110 Pegaso Z102s were built between 1951 and 1958, with vee-8 engines varying from 2.5-liter/140bhp to 3.2-liter/275bhp.

CHAPTER 2

1960s

Not only did supercar top speeds edge up towards 170mph during the 1960s, but the first mid-engined types (Lamborghini Miura and Ferrari Dino 206GT), and the first truly wind-cheating shapes (Jaguar E-Type) appeared. The Italian firms Iso and Maserati also burst onto the supercar manufacturing scene, as genuine rivals to Ferrari.

This specially-styled type of Ferrari 250GT (by Pininfarina) became rare in the 1960s, as series-production of other Ferraris began. Elegance, however, would never be lacking in the cream of Italian supercars.

Above: The AC Cobra looked muscular and powerful when standing still—the bulbous wheelarches made sure of that. The roll hoop behind the driver is not standard.

Left: Sometimes described as an AC Ace on steroids, the Cobra had massively flared wheelarches, fat tires, and that strange circular fender hiding away in the air intake.

Far left: This Cobra has extra wide wheels with a unique type of single nut fixing, and a roll hoop behind the driver's head.

Classic Profile

AC COBRA

Texan Carroll Shelby obviously believed the American axiom: "There's no substitute for cubic engines." His solution to making a real car out of the 2-liter AC Ace was to install a 4.7-liter Ford-USA vee-8 engine and call it the Cobra. The transformation was remarkable. The Ace had been a brisk, well-mannered, British sports car, but the Cobra became a bellowing, extrovert supercar. From 1965, with a revised chassis, and an even more powerful 7.0-liter Ford-USA engine, this car became the most exciting of all Anglo-American hybrids.

Although production of the AC Cobra officially ended in 1968, clones, copies, and re-creations have been on sale ever since, and modern ACs still use the same basic layout.

The car featured on this and the opposite page is a contemporary model from the United Kingdom.

Right: The Cobra instrument panel packed in as much information as possible.

Right: No-one could mistake a Cobra from this angle, for the style was unique.

Left: There were no concessions to ephemeral style at the rear of the Cobra, for all was purpose, and function. Those tires were need to deal with a lot of brute USA horsepower.

Cobras looked best of all when decked
out, ready to go motor racing. Even faster
on the track than on the road, they were
formidable competitors at all levels.

Left: De Tomaso's mid-engined Mangusta, first seen in 1967, carried a startling style. Powered by a 4.7-liter Ford-USA vee-8 engine, it could get up to more than 150mph.

Above: The Mangusta was a very attractive mid-engined two-seater. Hidden away under the skin was a steel backbone chassis. The shape was by Ghia.

Right: With 305bhp in the engine bay, and as a car which weighed little more than 2,900lb, the Mangusta needed fat tires to keep everything in check!

Left: The Ferrari 500 Superfast had a lushly trimmed cabin, really laid out for two (though others could just about squeeze in behind those fold-forward seats)—all intended for great comfort on long journeys. Air conditioning and power steering were both options.

Right: The Ferrari 500 Superfast's nose, by Pininfarina, was similar to that of several other Ferraris. In this case, the registration number gives a clue to the model type.

Right: Hidden away under that air cleaner is a 400bhp, 4.9-liter, vee-12 engine. In the 500 Superfast this guaranteed a top speed of up to 180mph.

Left: Pininfarina's artistry somehow made the big and bulky Ferrari 500 Superfast look delicate. Once the 4.9-liter engine was fired up, however, there was no mistaking its character. Only 36 cars were built in two years.

Right: Bertone produced the style for the Iso Fidia, which was one of that rare breed—a four-door supercar. With a 5.3-liter GM vee-8 engine, its chassis layout was closely related to the Grifo coupe.

Left: The 350GT was the very first Lamborghini to go on sale, in 1964. Lamborghini developed its own four-cam vee-12 engine, which produced 280bhp. The style was by Touring.

Right: The Lamborghini name was new to motor cars in 1963, the founder Ferruccio Lamborghini having already made his fortune in tractor production.

Below: Touring's long, sweeping lines for the 350GT hid a new tubular chassis which Giotto Bizzarrini had developed. This was a 150mph car, with all-independent suspension and a magnificent engine.

Left: This six-cylinder engined Maserati 3500GTi of the early 1960s was the first Italian supercar to have a fuel-injected engine.

Right: Some manufacturers announce their models in a very discreet manner. This Aston Martin "Vantage" badge proves the point.

Left: Frua was an independent Italian body builder who supplied versions of this coupe shape to more than one customer. This car is the Ford-USA engined AC 428, which used a longer version of the Cobra chassis.

FERRARI DINO

The Dino 206 of 1967 was the first of a completely new type of small Ferrari. Officially, at first, these were all called "Dino" (and not "Ferrari")—Dino being the name of Enzo Ferrari's first-born son.

The Dinos were the first Maranello road cars to use vee-6 engines, the first to have engines behind the seats, and the first to have transversely-mounted engines. The aluminum-

Above: The cockpit of the little Dino was well equipped and purposeful.

Left: A new name for a small Ferrari —"Dino" being the christian name of Enzo Ferrari's first-born son.

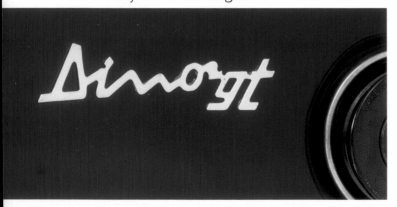

bodied 206 gave way to the 2.4-liter engined steel-bodied 246 in 1969, in a family which sold strongly until 1973, when the larger Dino 308 family arrived. In every way except price, this car was a competitor for the Porsche 911.

Above : Ferrari's first mid-engined road-car, the Dino, had a flawless Pininfarina style, which was remarkably similar to earlier Dino racing sports cars. This was the start of a distinguished Ferrari line.

Right: A new outlook on a new type of Ferrari— the first Ferrari road car with a mid-mounted engine. The style neatly hid the transverse engine under a slatted cover.

SPECIFICATIONS (246GT)

Engine	2,417cc/147.5cu.in
Horsepower	195@7,600rpm
Top speed	148mph/238kph)
Wheelbase	92.0in (234cm)
Weight	2,609lb (1,183kg)
Sales	2,487

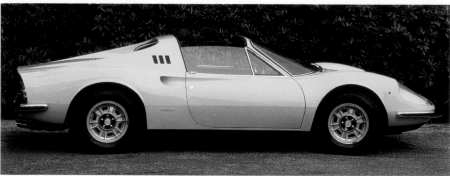

Left: Early Dinos were closed coupes, but a 246GTS (S="Spyder") with a removable roof panel was later added.

Right: The Dino 246GTS had an ideal driving position, in which the driver could lean well back from that famous steering wheel, and its equally legendary badge.

Far right: Pininfarina's elegant solution to the need for swept back panels on each side of the Dino engine deck, was to fit a wrap around sheet of glass between the cabin and the engine lid itself.

Left: Dino 246GTS types were usually driven with the roof panel removed, and stowed.

FERRARI 250GT BERLINETTA

Ferrari's 250GT Berlinetta was one of the most famous cars ever built. Although practical for road use, it was really meant to go motor racing. Some cars had steel bodies and were used on the road, but most were panelled in light alloy. It was a front-engined vee-12 without compromise, with a short-wheelbase version of the rigid tubular chassis, and with a 280bhp version of that legendary 3-liter vee-12 engine. Most Berlinettas were simply furnished, noisy to drive, but were amazingly effective.

Until the 275GTB came along (complete with its all-independent suspension chassis) this was one of the most nimble, and most desirable, of all Ferraris. Pininfarina could surely be proud of creating this unique shape.

Above right: Everything in the cabin of the 250GT Berlinetta was functional.

Right: This detail shows the simple style and front grille, and lack of fenders.

Left: This car has a snap action fuel filler cap, to save valuable seconds at race refuelling stops.

Classic Pininfarina lines of the 1960s.

Most of the tail on a Berlinetta was occupied by a vast gas tank.

SPECIFICATIONS

Engine	2,953cc/180.3cu.in
Horsepower	280@7,000rpm
Top speed	150mph (241kph)
Wheelbase	94.5in (240.0cm)
Weight	2,110lb (957kg)
Sales	167

Left: Aston Martin's DB6 was really a longer-wheelbase version of the DB5, with a more spacious cabin, but with no loss of performance. In every respect this was a match for contemporary four-seater Ferraris, and it sold extremely well.

Right: Compared with the DB5, the Aston Martin DB6 had a longer wheelbase, more space in the cabin, and a new rear-end style with a spoiler to help high-speed stability.

Below: Ferrari's 250GTO had a no-nonsense driving position, where function always came ahead of style and glamor. The rev-counter in the middle of the facia display was there to warn enthusiastic drivers of over-revving.

Right: In the 1960s, every sportsman's idea of bliss was to drive a Ferrari 250GTO. According to the sporting regulations, this was a road car, but every one of the 42 cars made was used in motor racing at one time or another.

Opposite top: The Iso Grifo was launched in 1965, with power by a 300bhp/5.3-liter Chevrolet Corvette power unit.

Left: Over the years, the Iso Grifo was built with several different types of Chevrolet vee-8 engine.

Above: The extra louvers and "penthouse" roof on the 7-liter Grifo were needed to clear the extra bulk of the largest 7-liter Chevrolet vee-8 engine.

Opposite bottom: Before designing the Iso Grifo, Giotti Bizzarrini developed an eponymous sports coupe, introduced in 1965.

Right: Bertone worked his particular magic on the large and impressive four-seater Lamborghini Espada, which was announced in 1968, and featured a front-mounted 4.0-liter/vee-12 engine which produced no less than 325bhp.

Left: Bertone's artistry was pushed to the limit when it was asked to clothe a four-seater Lamborghini cabin inside a fashionable two-door body shape in 1968.

Right: Several Bertone styling "cues" are obvious in the shape of the original Lamborghini Espada: four headlamps fitted into a full-width front grille; the sweep-up of the line under the glass on the side of the shell; and the very high tail proportions popular during this period.

Left: Maserati produced this, the original two-seater Ghibli coupe, in 1966. Ghia styled the shell, which covered a front-engine/rear-drive chassis with a choice of 4.2-liter or 4.7-liter vee-8 engines.

Right: Italian stylists learned much about air-smoothing, and sexy shapes, during the 1960s. Compared with any earlier Maserati, this sinuous Ghia-styled Ghibli was more integrated.

Below: Car designers from Italy always looked after tiny detail to set their stamp on a particular vehicle.

Bottom right: The trident badge was Maserati's own, and Ghibli was the name of a hot desert wind in Africa.

Above: It was only if the manufacturer was proud of your work that a styling house was allowed to put its name on the side of a new product. Maserati was pleased with what Ghia had done on the Ghibli, so this was the result.

Left: Was this Ghia-styled car, the Maserati Ghibli of 1966, as attractive as the Ferrari Daytona which followed it two years later?

Right: The Maserati Ghibli was introduced in 1966, and sold steadily until 1973, by which times no fewer than 1,274 examples—coupe and Spyder— had been delivered.

FERRARI 275GTB

Except for its 3.3-liter vee-12 engine, everything about the Ferrari 275GTB was new. This was the very first Ferrari road car to use a multi-tube chassis frame, which featured independent suspension at front and rear, and the first to have a rear-mounted five-speed gearbox in unit with the final drive. The Pininfarina style made much of the new engineering.

275GTBs were made from 1964 to 1968. Early cars had a short nose and a single-cam 280bhp vee-12 engine, but from 1966 (this shape), the nose was lengthened, and the vee-12 given twin-cam heads. With no less than 300bhp, here was a fantastic car which could reach nearly 160mph. Many were used in motorsport, which was surely the original intended use for this proud car.

Above: The 275GTB's mighty 300bhp vee-12 engine.

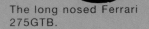

The long nosed Ferrari 275GTB.

SPECIFICATIONS

Engine	3,286cc/200.6cu.in
Horsepower	300@8,000rpm
Top speed	155mph (250kph)
Wheelbase	94.5in (240.0 cm)
Weight	2,490lb (1,129kg)
Sales	455

Above:
Pininfarina
shaped every
Ferrari road car
in the 1960s.

Right: The
275GTB's cabin
was modern,
comfortable, and
nicely detailed.

Right: The forest of brightly-chromed wheel spokes, the functional cooling slots in the front wings, and the famous yellow Prancing Horse transfer badge all add up to one obvious identification—another famous Ferrari. This, in fact, is a 275GTB/4.

Left: There are several elegant Pininfarina styling cues in this Ferrari 275GTB/4 which were shared with other such Ferraris of the period. These included that conically-curved nose, and the vast fairings over the headlamps. But not a line out of place, and no surplus decoration, either.

Below: Aston Martin established the new DBS line in 1967, first with the existing six-cylinder engine, and from 1969 with the brand-new vee-8.

Right: The lines of the Aston Martin DBS family—this was a six-cylinder-engined Vantage—hid a full four-seater cabin.

Far right: Like all other Isos, the Lele was a front- (Chevrolet vee-8) engined machine, closely related to other, similar types.

Above: Lamborghini's Islero was a simply-styled car, with these neat flip-up headlamps. The full-width front fender and the shallow outlet mounted low down were tidy features.

Left: The Lamborghini Islero featured a new two-seater coupe body shell, by Marazzi of Milan, all mounted on the existing 350GT/4000GT chassis.

Right: The instrument display of the Lamborghini Islero. The two instruments that matter most—speedometer and engine rev counter—are right in front of the driver's eyes.

Below: From 1963 to 1969, Maserati built the smart Mistral coupe, with a close-coupled four-seater style by Frua. This particular style featured a hatchback, and was built on the chassis and running gear of the six-cylinder engined Sebring. With a choice of 245bhp/3,692cc or 255bhp/4,012cc, this was a 140mph car.

Right: Maserati's Mistral was an understated supercar, with a choice of fuel-injected, six-cylinder engines. There was also an open-top Spider version. In six years, no fewer than 948 of both types were built.

Above: Maserati's Trident
trademark was—and still is—
one of the most famous Italian
supercar badges of all.

FERRARI 365 GTB/4 DAYTONA

In 1968 the new Ferrari 365 GTB/4 Daytona was certainly the fastest front-engined car in the world. The combination of a 352bhp/4.4-liter vee-12 engine, and a wind-cheating Pininfarina two-seater coupe style, was irresistible. Tests showed that it could reach near 175mph, and some owners have claimed more. Mechanically, it was related to the last of the 275GTB/4 types, though it had a new and larger type of engine, and it would reign supreme at Ferrari until 1974, when it was finally replaced by the mid-engined Boxer.

Pundits who could never afford to own a Daytona complained that it was heavy to drive, but owners just smiled and enjoyed their magnificent two-seaters. Developed as a road car, with many creature comforts, the Daytona could also be drastically lightened and turned into a racing coupe.

SPECIFICATIONS

Engine	4,390cc/268cu.in
Horsepower	352@7,500rpm
Top speed	174mph (280kph)
Wheelbase	94.5in (240.0cm)
Weight	3,530lb (1,600kg)
Sales	1,406 all models

Above: The Daytona engine was a superlative piece of Ferrari engineering.

Right: In 1968, the Daytona's style brought gasps of admiration.

Left: The 250GT Lusso of 1962 to 1964 was one of the most civilized front-vee-12 engined Ferraris ever built. It was an ideal foil for the more extrovert SWB Berlinetta of the period— sophisticated instead of brutal, silky instead of forceful, but still quite beautiful.

Right: Ferrari cabins, facia layouts, and instrument displays altered only slowly as the 1960s passed—all of them offering mounds of information, and all of them with that legendary Prancing Horse badge on the horn push.

Far left: The Ferrari 365 California of the mid-1960s was another Spyder whose title described exactly where Ferrari hoped it would sell. With 320bhp from 4.4-liters, it was an exciting way to go topless in hot-climate conditions.

Left: Old fashioned today? Maybe, but in the 1960s, the most fashionable way to go supercar motoring was to have center-lock wire wheels. On a 365 California there were big three-ear spinners to hold them in place.

Left: Only 14 365 California were produced in 1966 and 1967, only two of them having right-hand-drive. This made these supercars at once astonishingly rare, desirable, and eventually very valuable indeed.

Right: Only two seats in a Ferrari of that size? Point out that it was wasteful of space, and every Ferrari enthusiast in the world will merely laugh at you. It was image, style, and presence which mattered, after all.

Left: The Ferrari 250GT Lusso of 1962 to 1964 was a pleasing style from any angle. Not only was it a beautiful car, but it was the most practical and useable of all Ferrari road cars at this time.

Right: Does any more need to be said? The Ferrari "prancing horse" badge, and the name, starkly spelt out, was all one needed to identify one of the world's most charismatic supercars.

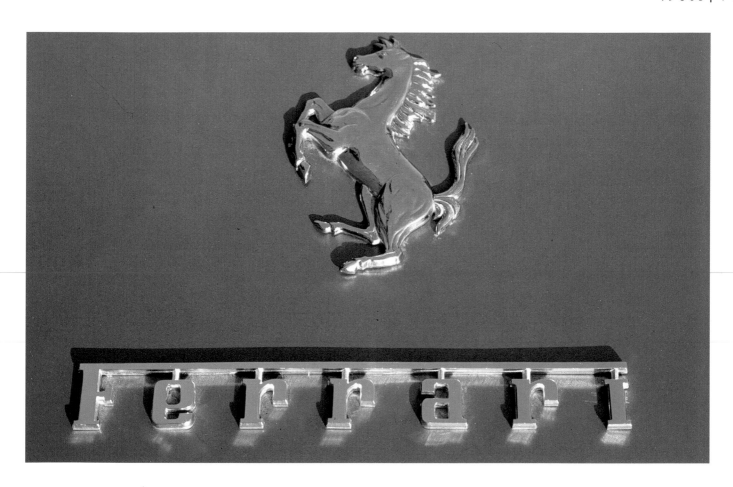

Left: Ferrari's 330GTC was built from 1965 to 1967. Less highly-tuned than the 275GTB of the day, it shared that car's chassis, but had 2+2 seating and a single-cam-per-bank vee-12 engine.

Right: The long hood of the Ferrari 330GTC hid a single-overhead-cam per bank 300bhp/4.0-liter engine. More of a "touring" than a "sporting" supercar, it was a well-equipped, high-speed, long-distance road car which could reach 143mph.

Below: Although rare, Ferrari 400 Superamericas came in all shapes and sizes. This particular Pininfarina theme was styled on the longer of the two wheelbases, and was always known by the name "Coupe Aerodinamico."

Above: Yet another impressive Ferrari instrument display, this one being of the "Coupe Aerodinamico" 400 Superamerica.

Right: The "Coupe Aerodinamico" style on the Ferrari 400 Superamerica of the 1960s was popular with the clientele—no fewer than 31 of the 48 400 Superamericas ever built had this distinctive style.

JAGUAR E-TYPE

No new supercar caused quite such a sensation as the Jaguar E-Type at its launch in 1961. Not only was it beautiful, but aerodynamically efficient. Not only was it advertised as a 150mph machine, but it was to be sold at such an amazingly low price.

In the beginning, the E-Type was meant to be a racing replacement for the famous D-Type racing sports car. Soon, though, the idea of making it a successor to the long-running XK series took hold. Accordingly, though it kept the same basic style and chassis as conceived, it was given a larger-capacity engine in road-car tune, a full-size windshield, and a choice of two-seater open sports or fastback/hatchback coupe shapes.

Sensationally styled, the E-Type was one of the world's most recognizable cars. This car is a late-1960s Series II type.

Left: Like the D-Type which it followed, the superbly streamlined Jaguar E-Type was always intended to cheat the wind.

Above: Practical features of the E-Type coupe included a hatchback on the tail, and very neat packaging at the rear.

Early cars had 265bhp/3.8-liter XK engines, and could reach 150mph. From 1964, a more torquey 4.2-liter engine was fitted, a 2+2 coupe was developed, and as the years passed the E-Type became more civilized and better-equipped.

Left: All Jaguar E-types had a compact, and rather slim, driving compartment.

Right: The entire front-end of a Jaguar E-Type's bodywork lifted up to provide engine bay access.

SPECIFICATIONS

Engine	4,235cc/258.5cu.in
Horsepower	265@5,400rpm
Top speed	153mph (246kph)
Wheelbase	96.0in (243.8cm)
Weight	2,800lb (1,270kg)
Sales	57,230 (6-cyl cars)

Every line, profile,
and contour of the
Jaguar E-Type was
aimed at reducing
the aerodynamic
drag of the car, and
styling—as such—
came second. This
early-spec. car
shows the cowled
headlamps, the slim
front and rear
fenders, and the
smoothly-detailed
under-side.

LAMBORGHINI MIURA

When launched in 1966, Lamborghini's Miura set a completely new supercar standard. Not only was it the world's first mid/rear-engined supercar, but it was the first to have a vee-12 engine mounted transversely across the chassis.

The Miura was very fast—even in the beginning, with a 350bhp/4.0-liter vee-12 it could approach 170mph—and its Bertone-styled looks were simply sensational. Because of its layout, and especially because of its new-kid-on-the-block character, it put Ferrari into disarray, and it was years before that Italian rival got back on terms.

Miuras were not perfect—those brave enough to drive them flat out suggest that there was a tendency for the nose to lift as

SPECIFICATIONS

Engine	3,929cc/240cu.in
Horsepower	385@7,850rpm
Top speed	170mph (274kph)
Wheelbase	98.4in (250.0cm)
Weight	2,850lb (1,293kg)
Sales	763, all types

Above: The Miura SV was the final, 385bhp, version of this world-famous supercar.

Right: The massive mid/rear-mounted vee-12 engine of the Miura.

maximum speed approached—but they were, quite simply, unique, and there was a constant stream of orders. The first major change was to the 400S of 1970, which had 370bhp, and the final derivative was the even-better developed 400SV (shown here), which had 385bhp, and could almost certainly approach 180mph.

Left: The Miura's headlamps cleverly flipped up, then the lights came on.

Below: The nose air intakes were for radiators and front-end cooling.

Right: The Miura's body engineering featured entire lift-up sections.

Right: All Miura production cars carried the same two-seater closed-coupe style, complete with flip-up headlamps and alloy wheels.

Far right: The Miura looked exactly right, perfectly proportioned even, from every angle. How did they package that 4-liter vee-12 engine so neatly?

Below: Bertone-watchers can probably pick out one or two styling "cues" from contemporary rivals such as the Iso Grifo, but the Miura was always unmistakeable.

Left: Introduced in 1967, Ferrari's 365GT 2+2 was its first almost-four-seater to have all-independent suspension. Because this was more "road car" than "racing sports car," the chassis was simpler than that of the contemporary 275GTB/4. By any standards, this was a physically large Ferrari.

Right: TVR's mid-1960s Griffith 400 might not look like a supercar, but the engine bay hid a mighty 271bhp/4.7-liter Ford-USA vee-8, and it could exceed 150mph with some ease. This was a light car, with a multi-tube frame, and all-independent suspension.

CHAPTER 3

1970s

Although the 1970s was darkened by the Yom Kippur War, and two serious Energy Crises, there was a rash of new supercars. More and more political restrictions could not stifle magnificent turbocharged Porsches, the new Ferrari Boxer, and a host of fresh Lamborghinis and Maseratis. These were fascinating times for all automotive enthusiasts.

Porsche's new 911 Turbo set new supercar standards in the 1970s—not just by its performance, but by the quality of its engineering. Attention to detail, competent aerodynamics, and well-developed engines offered an unbeatable combination for a time.

Above: Aston Martin's Lagonda saloon offered more electronic displays than any previous car. The cabin, its equipment, and style were all new.

Far right: Challenged to provide a "new" look for the Aston Martin Lagonda, stylist William Towns produced this amazing shape.

Right: The Lagonda was a sharp-edged marvel. Even the headlamps were rectangular, and only the wheels were round.

ASTON MARTIN VANTAGE

Ten years after the original Aston Martin DBS had appeared, the factory treated it to a monstrously powerful (380bhp) 5.3-liter version of the modern vee-8. This was the Vantage model, which could reach 170mph in great stability, and apparently with little fuss and bother. As British as a bulldog, the Vantage produced its shattering performance with little of the spectacular sound of an Italian supercar, for it was heavy and sturdy rather than sexy, with practical rather than high-tech. engineering.

Yet this was a car which could carry four passengers in rather close-coupled comfort, with air-conditioning to keep them cool, and with wood and high-quality carpet to cosset them in luxury. It was only the bellowing vee-8 engine, and the rather brusque character, which reminded anyone that this was perhaps the old fashioned way to provide truly high performance.

From this angle it would be easy to miss the fact that the Vantage was a four-seater supercar, but this was indeed a rather large, certainly, wide machine.

The massive bulge in the hood was needed to provide clearance over the bulky vee-8 engine of the Aston Martin Vantage. In spite of its size, this was a remarkably nimble car to drive, flexible yet amazingly fast.

SPECIFICATIONS

Engine	5,340cc/326cu.in
Horsepower	380@6,000rpm
Top speed	170mph (274kph)
Wheelbase	102.7in (261.0cm)
Weight	4,000lb (1,814kg)
Sales	3,228 (all DBS/V8s)

Left: To keep the Vantage well-balanced at high speeds, Aston Martin provided a large under-fender "chin spoiler." At the same time, the normal radiator grille opening was blanked off, for tests proved that little cooling air got in that way!

Right: From this angle the Vantage looks bulky and substantial. In fact it was quite a large car, and with such sharp-edged shaping it was difficult to disguise that fact. Traditional British engineering, in fact, at its best.

Above: Considering that the De Tomaso Pantera was an amalgam of Italian engineering, a contract styling job by Ghia, and a Ford-USA vee-8 engine, the result was an extremely integrated machine.

Left: The De Tomaso Pantera's cabin was so typical of Italian supercars of the 1970s period.

Right: Ghia did a great job, for the Pantera was a very pleasing style from all angles.

Left: The de Tomaso Pantera was a project inspired by Ford-USA, who encouraged the Italians to evolve a two-seater supercar which could be sold through the Lincoln-Mercury dealer chain. This worked well, but only for two or three years altogether.

Right: When the new mid-engined Dino 308GT4 arrived in 1973, it was the very first Ferrari-designed road car to use a vee-8 power unit, and the first to use a Bertone style. Within two years this 2+2-seater would be overshadowed by the two-seater Pininfarina coupe version which would follow.

Below: When Pininfarina styled the Dino 308GTB/GTS family, he started a family which would sell extremely well for the next 13 years. This is the GTS, from 1977.

Right: With the rigid roof panel bolted back into place, the 308 GTS once again became a snug two-seater coupe. This was a very successful derivative in warm-climate countries.

Left: When Jaguar treated the E-Type to a new vee-12 engine in 1971—thus evolving the Series III—it meant that the front grille had to be enlarged, the wheels had to become fatter, and the wheel arches had to be flared. Still a great-looking car, though.

Far left: From the rear, you could always identify the E-Type Series III by its fatter wheels and rear arches.

Below: For the Series III E-Type, Jaguar pushed the headlamps slightly farther forward in their recesses.

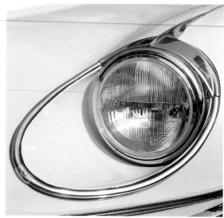

Above: Jaguar somehow inserted the big 60-deg. Vee-12 engine into the engine bay of the E-Type—and managed to keep it cool.

Left: The end of the road for the E-Type. This was the very last of the E-Type line, a Series III Roadster built in the winter of 1974/1975.

Right: From this angle it is difficult to see that this E-Type is a Series III, but the wider wheels and flared arches give it away.

Left: By comparison with other Lamborghinis which were being made at the time, the front-engined 2+2 seater Jarama S, with style by Bertone, was a rather craggy-looking machine.

Left: Under the Bertone-styled skin of the Jarama S there was a 365bhp/4.0-liter vee-12 engine— exactly as fitted to current mid-engined Miuras. The Jarama S could easily reach 160mph, and was more than a match for its competitors.

Right: Original Jaramas did not need the extra air outlets in the flanks, nor the extra air intake scoop on the hood.

Above: Lancia's tiny mid-Ferrari-engined Stratos was conceived with world-class rallying in mind.

Left: With the power of the Stratos all in the tail, there was space in the wedge nose only for the spare wheel, and the passengers' footwells.

Right: The Lancia Stratos was a minimum-size supercar in all but character and results, for Bertone made it short, stubby, and with a very cramped cabin, to wrap it around the mid-Ferrari vee-6 engined tub. Skin panels were all in fiberglass.

FERRARI 365GT4/BB "BOXER"

No-one ever thought of this fabulous new Ferrari as anything other than the "Boxer." Ferrari might have wanted it to be known as the 365GT4/BB, but no enthusiast was ever going to use that soulless acronym. Because this new car had a flat twelve engine, everyone used the "Boxer" nickname, which was already applied to other less famous "flat" engines.

In Ferrari's long-term scheme of things, here was a direct replacement for the much-loved Daytona, but a car different in every way. The engine was behind instead of in front of the

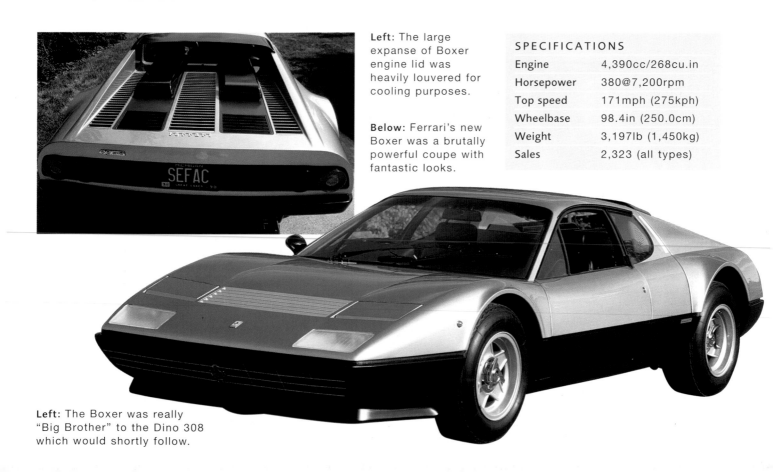

Left: The large expanse of Boxer engine lid was heavily louvered for cooling purposes.

Below: Ferrari's new Boxer was a brutally powerful coupe with fantastic looks.

SPECIFICATIONS

Engine	4,390cc/268cu.in
Horsepower	380@7,200rpm
Top speed	171mph (275kph)
Wheelbase	98.4in (250.0cm)
Weight	3,197lb (1,450kg)
Sales	2,323 (all types)

Left: The Boxer was really "Big Brother" to the Dino 308 which would shortly follow.

driver, the layout completely fresh—and at last Ferrari had a mid/rear-engined car to fight with against their Italian rivals.

The styling, of course, came from Pininfarina, and even without badging its Ferrari purpose was always evident.

Left: Simple circular stop and tail lamps were typical of 1970s' Ferraris.

Below: For access to the engine bay of the Boxer, lift up the entire rear section.

Right: The Boxer had a more modest size of "transmission" tunnel than many.

Above: When Lotus turbocharged the 2.2-liter Esprit, it thought that no more than a single, discreet badge, was needed. The performance did the rest.

Left: The mystery of inspecting a supercar is knowing what lies behind every grille, every slot, or every louver. Be sure, though, that it all has a purpose.

Right: The Italian stylist, Giorgetto Giugiaro, shaped the original Lotus Esprit, which went on sale in 1976. The first turbocharged version followed in 1980.

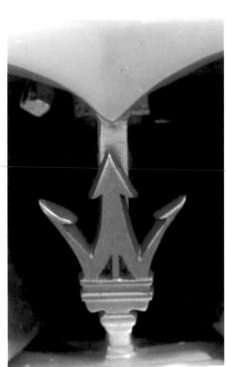

Left: The Lotus Esprit Turbo looked right from every angle. Apart from a larger front spoiler, and sills under the door, this looked almost the same as the original normally-aspirated machine of 1976.

Above: Maserati took their time before joining in with a mid/rear-engined supercar. This eventually appeared in 1971, as the much respected, and very rapid, 160mph Bora.

Right: Unlike Ferrari, Maserati made slight stylistic changes to their famous "Trident" as the years passed by, but identification was never in doubt.

Above: By the 1970s, stylists had found elegant ways of integrating every feature of the front of a fast car. This was the front of the Maserati Bora, Maserati's first and only mid-vee-8 engined supercar.

Right: Maserati very neatly linked the roof of the Bora to the tail by using a long slanting buttress.

Far right: Two different Maseratis were developed from this same chunky shape—the Bora, with a vee-8 engine, like this car, and the slightly less powerful vee-6 engined Merak. However, there were still differences around the rear quarters.

Left: By the early 1980s, the Ferrari 308GTB had been given a fuel injected engine, and a quattrovalvole (four-valve) derivative would follow that, but there was never any need to alter the original 1970s style.

Right: Ferrari's 308GTB clustered all its instruments in a binnacle ahead of the driver's eyes, while the central "services" tunnel not only accepted the gear shift and the handbrake, but windshield wiper, heater, and other minor controls, too.

Below: The Ferrari 308GTS was a very popular openable-top derivative of the original Dino 308GTB. The roof panel was designed to be unclipped (as here), and stowed away.

Right: Plain to some, the 308GT4 was Bertone's take on what a genuine two-plus-two coupe, with the vee-8 engine mounted behind the cabin, should look like.

Above: Lamborghini's first attempt at providing a "small" supercar came in 1970 with this neat little Urraco. This was totally different from the existing vee-12 types, for it had a lightweight 90-degree vee-8 engine mounted behind the cabin.

Left: Lamborghini's new Urraco was graced with a body style by Bertone, which somehow squeezed 2+2 seating into a package no more than 13 feet long. Because the engine was in the tail, the nose could be low, and have very few air intakes.

Right: At first it does not look feasible, but Bertone somehow managed to provide 2+2 seating (not full four-seater by any means though) into the Lamborghini Urraco cabin. Even in its original form, with a 182bhp/2.0-liter engine, this pretty little machine could reach nearly 145mph.

Right: The Maserati Indy, built from 1969 to 1975, was one of a sequence of fine, practical, and successful front-engined Maseratis. Fitted with a big vee-8 engine, it was a unit-construction 2+2-seater which fitted between the Ghibli and Mexico models in the Maserati range. The style was by Vignale, one of the last efforts from that independent company.

Left: As was the Italian fashion at that time, the tail of the Maserati Indy was high, and sharply cut off. Those twin exhaust outlets are there for a purpose, for an Indy was sold with 260bhp/4.2-liter or 330bhp/4.7-liter vee-8 engines.

Right: Vignale's style on the Maserati Indy hid that company's big, robust, and very simply engineered twin-cam-per-bank vee-8 engine. With the 330bhp unit installed, a top speed of 156mph was possible in this car.

Above: Based on the chassis of the Daytona, Ferrari's 365 GTC/4 was one of the most successful interim supercars. Although it was only made in 1971 and 1972, this 340bhp/4.4-liter machine attracted no fewer than 500 customers in all.

Right: As ever, Pininfarina produced this Ferrari style. In some ways the 365 GTC/4 looked like the existing Daytona, but it had a bigger cabin, with 2+2 seating. This car could easily beat 150mph.

Left: The rear of the Ferrari 365 GTC/4 looked rather like that of the even larger 365 GT 2+2 which was soon to follow. Pininfarina never wasted a successful theme on only one car.

Designed to replace the Indy, the new Maserati Khamsin of 1972 was one of Bertone's most wickedly aggressive wedge-nose styles. Hidden away there was a 320bhp/4.9-liter version of Maserati's long-running four-cam vee-8. The Khamsin was so carefully shaped that it could reach 160mph.

LAMBORGHINI COUNTACH

In the 1970s the mid-engined Countach was, quite simply, the fastest of all the Italian Supercars. Even in its original form, with a 375bhp/4.0-liter vee-12 engine, it could beat 180mph, a rate not to be beaten by any Ferrari or Maserati of the period.

To replace the Miura, Lamborghini had to produce something sensational, and the Countach was that car. Now with a square-section tubular frame, and with its vee-12 engine longitudinally mounted, this was a bigger car than the Miura, and carried a dazzling Bertone style. The basic shape was hard-edged, with a low nose, but the unique feature was the lift-up doors which hinged upwards, insect fashion, towards the front of the car. Parking width, therefore, was never a problem, though it was difficult to remain anonymous when exiting such a flamboyant machine.

The doors of the Countach hinged upward, and swung forward when operated —a unique feature not adopted on any other car up to this moment. The nose was ultra-low, the engine behind the cabin.

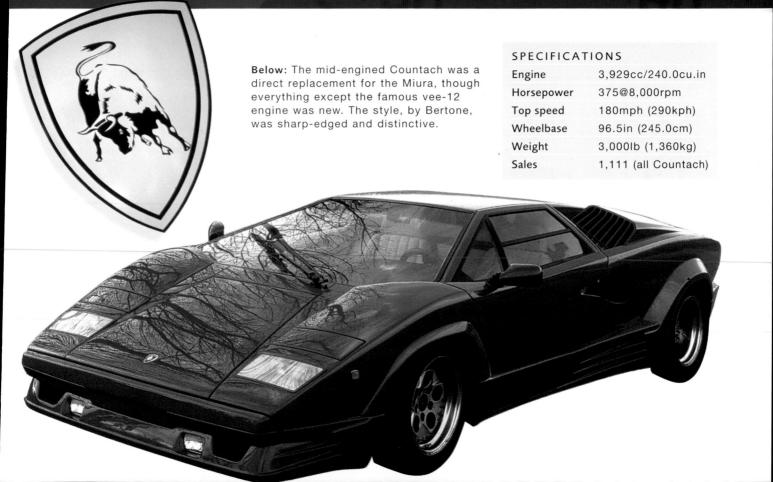

Below: The mid-engined Countach was a direct replacement for the Miura, though everything except the famous vee-12 engine was new. The style, by Bertone, was sharp-edged and distinctive.

SPECIFICATIONS

Engine	3,929cc/240.0cu.in
Horsepower	375@8,000rpm
Top speed	180mph (290kph)
Wheelbase	96.5in (245.0cm)
Weight	3,000lb (1,360kg)
Sales	1,111 (all Countach)

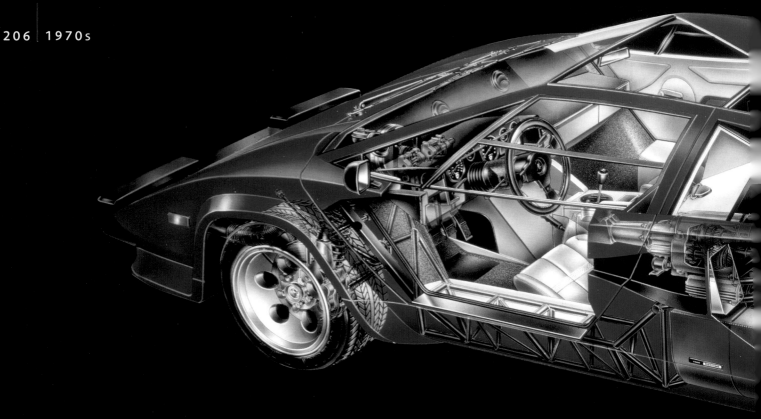

The Countach was a gloriously complex supercar, for its square-tube chassis frame had the massive vee-12 engine, which was behind the two-seater cabin, the monstrously fast wheels and tires, all in a minimum-dimension steel/alloy body shell. It was only a two-seater of course, and the ultimate high-performance road car of its day.

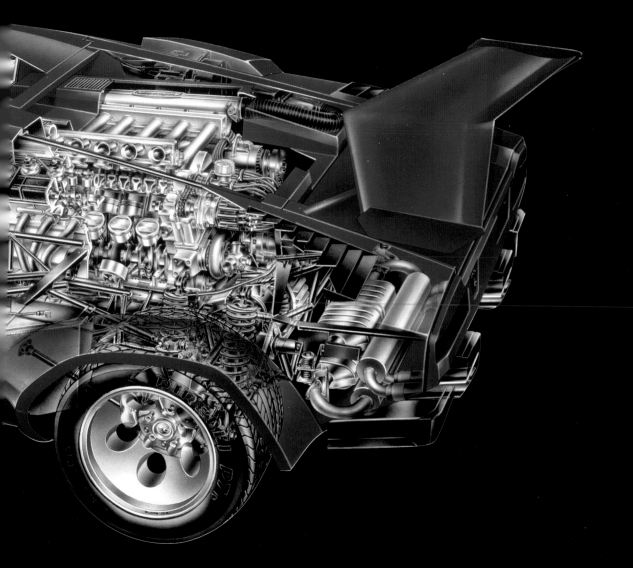

Above: Lamborghini's Countach looked impressive from any angle. Those seeing one for the first time were often surprised by its bulk, which Bertone's styling expertise hid very well.

Right: Although the Lamborghini Countach was quite a sizeable car, it had only a narrow two-seater cabin. The view from inside was just as impressive as that from outside the nose...

Above: Porsche offered a "Sport Equipment" body package for their fastest 911, which included a hidden-headlamp nose, and these louvers, which helped to channel hot air out from the front brake region.

Left: Starting in the mid-1970s, Porsche introduced, then continued to develop, a turbocharged version of the 911. In the next two decades, there would be continual change to this seminal German supercar.

Right: The "Sport Equipment" conversion on the 911 Turbo was a typically thorough re-development of the factory theme, with a lowered nose, extra cooling vents at front and rear, and deep sills along the flanks. These cars were very rare, and very desirable.

PORSCHE 911 TURBO

Porsche's 911 Turbo changed the face of supercar motoring. Not only was this a very fast Porsche, but it was engineered with typically German thoroughness. Until 1975, supercars had been forgiven a few faults and failings, but once the 911 Turbo was launched, these could not be tolerated.

All 911 Turbos had rear-mounted, flat-six, air-cooled engines. The first examples had 260bhp/3.0-liter engines, the first 300bhp/3.3-liter types appeared in 1977, and development continued steadily thereafter.

Before the late-1990s, when the last was made, a four-wheel-drive version had arrived, suspension was much improved, and 3.6-liter engines had been boosted to produce 360bhp. Much more was available for motorsport.

Right: The massive "whale-tail" spoiler of the 911 Turbo was strictly functional, for it provided much needed down-force at higher road speeds.

Maybe the lines of the late-1970s 911 Turbo were not as pure as the original, but every change—wide wheels, wide arches, and deep front spoiler included—were there for a purpose.

SPECIFICATIONS

Engine	3,299cc/201.4cu.in
Horsepower	300@5,500rpm
Top speed	160mph (257.4kph)
Wheelbase	89.4in (227.0cm
Weight	2,884lb (1,308kg)
Sales	Approx 30,000

Right: The original 911 had been styled without spoilers or extra add-ons, but the Turbo's big rear spoiler, the flared arches, and the wide-rim wheels made it look even more purposeful.

Right: The cabin of this Ferrari 400 GTi was as well-equipped as that of a light aircraft—the car cost as much, too. This was the first Ferrari, also, to be offered with optional automatic transmission, which proved to be very popular with Ferrari's customers.

Left: This was the Ferrari 400GTi of 1979, with a 310bhp/4.8-liter vee-12 engine. The original version, the 365 GT4 2+2, had been launched in 1972, with a 340bhp/4.4-liter power unit. Both cars could beat 150mph: there was an automatic version of the 400GT.

Below: Typically neat installation and styling detail of the pop-up headlamps in the 365GT4 2+2/400GTi saloon family.

Right: Purists suggested that Ferraris should never be four-seater saloons, but sales of this family—the 365 GT4 2+2 thru' 412i (1972 to 1989)—proved them wrong. In all that time, the style was never changed, but vee-12 engines were enlarged from 4.4-liter to 4.9-liters.

Left: Vee-12 engined Ferrari engine bays were always full of machinery, but when Bosch fuel injection was added for the 400GT in 1979, there was positively a maze of pipe-work, wiring and control gear up front. Note—this car has two separate Bosch injection distributors—one for each cylinder bank.

Below: The ultimate development of Ferrari's full four-seater saloon theme was the 412i model, built from 1985 to 1989. By this time it was a very sophisticated car, with a magnificent vee-12 engine and many creature comforts.

Right: Maserati's Kyalami, a 2+2-seater coupe, was styled by Frua, and first appeared in 1976. De Tomaso had recently taken control of Maserati, so it was reasonable that this car was based on the De Tomaso Longchamps.

Left: The Ferrari Mondial 8 first appeared in 1980 and, as a 2+2 seater on a longer wheelbase version of the existing mid-engined 308 chassis, took over directly from the 308 GT4. The Mondial had been styled by Pininfarina, and was at once more rounded, and a little larger than the earlier 308GT4. With 214bhp/2.9-liters at first, and 240bhp with four valve heads from 1982, it was a capable and compact car.

Above: Although the Maserati Bora was the first, and the last, of Maserati's big-mid-engined supercars, this vee-6 engined Merak was produced on the same basic platform. With slightly different rear quarter styling, and initially with a 190bhp/3.0-liter engine, this was the "entry-level" mid-engined Maserati, which could reach 135mph. Later types were more powerful, and faster.

Above: The Maserati Merak used a 90-degree vee-6 derivative of the famous vee-8, which was so much shorter that it was possible for Maserati to squeeze more space into the cabin. They claimed it was a 2+2 seater, although those in the rear could not have been very comfortable.

Right: The Merak, and its bigger brother, the Bora, were both handsome mid-engined Maseratis, with a style by Giugiaro. In the 1970s, most companies were agreed that they should position supercar engines behind the cabin, and their stylists were encouraged to evolve low, wedge-style, noses.

Above: Tail-lamp detailing of the Porsche 928, with the lenses tucked well away inside the rounded contours of the tail.

Left: Porsche designed the impressive front-engined 928 to take over from the 911, but it never worked out like that—both cars ran side-by-side with great success for many years.

Top right: The 928's original "mouse hole" wheels were distinctive, and were soon copied by other concerns. The Porsche shield badge on the center of the wheel was quite unmistakeable.

Right: For the 928, Porsche evolved a brand new 90-degree vee-8 engine—only their second all-new road-car engine in nearly 30 years.

CHAPTER 4

1980s

In the 1980s the supercar industry shrugged off all the gloom of the 1970s by launching a whole series of flamboyant new models. More of them got four-wheel-drive and cars like the Ferrari F40 finally approached top speeds of 200mph. Front-engined supercars virtually disappeared, and there were new names (Alpine-Renault and BMW among them), to challenge the Ferrari supremacy.

Ferrari's new turbocharged F40 was the most charismatic of all new supercars, with drop-dead gorgeous styling, and colossal, near-200mph, performance.

Above: Not only did the aluminum wheels of the Renault GTA look distinctive, but those vanes were there to encourage airflow over the disc brakes.

Left: In 1985 the new Renault Alpine GTA (or Alpine-Renault, as badged in some markets), was an impressive new supercar contender.

Right: The nose of the Renault Alpine GTA featured carefully faired headlamp units. This smart body was actually constructed of fiberglass, a traditional material for the Alpine concern of Dieppe, France, which assembled the cars.

Left: This Renault Alpine owner clearly wants the world to know that his vee-6 engine is turbocharged—the badging, need we say, was not as provided by the factory. Turbo Alpines could reach nearly 215mph.

Right: The Renault Alpine GTA Turbo featured a tail-mounted 200bhp/2.5-liter vee-6 engine. Even though the weight distribution was biased well toward the tail, this was a stable and very nimble supercar.

Left: The styling of the mid-1980s Renault Alpine was so beautifully carried out that it would be easy to miss the location of the vee-6 engine, which is in the extreme tail. Many people thought the Renault to be more attractive than the Porsche 911, with which it obviously competed.

Aston Martin's massive Virage coupe replaced the long-running V8 model at the end of the 1980s. Still based on a conventional front-engined layout, the Virage used a 32-valve evolution of the famous 5.3-liter vee-8 engine. Aston Martin claimed 330bhp from the 5.3-liter engine, which delivered this full four-seater saloon/coupe with a top speed of 157mph.

Below: BMW's mid-engined M1 was a fascinating amalgam of Italian flair and German engineering, for Lamborghini designed the chassis, and Ital Design developed the style, while final assembly was always in Germany. With a 277bhp/3.5-liter six-cylinder engine, the top speed of this car was 162mph.

Right: In a typically neat touch, BMW included their famous blue-and-white "spinner" badge into the corner of the engine bay cover, at the very tail of the M1. The M1 was carefully engineered, but very fast and responsive. For BMW, though, so few of this car were built that it was something of an irrelevance.

Right: Although there had been fast Chevrolet Corvettes in earlier years, the ZR-1 type of 1990, complete with its Lotus-designed four-cam 5.7-liter engine, was a genuine supercar.

Left: The Corvette ZR-1 looked good from any angle, and had an all-independent-suspension chassis to match the wind-cheating looks. American buyers had always loved Corvettes, not only for their made-at-home characters, but because they offered such remarkable value for money.

Right: Born in the USA in the mid-1980s, the Corvette was a famous, versatile, and very popular two-seater. Some owners preferred to own one with a coupe style—like this ZR-1—others loved the ever-popular drop-top alternative. When a Corvette was equipped with the Lotus-type 375bhp ZR-1 engine, here was a genuine 175mph machine.

FERRARI TESTAROSSA

Launched in 1984, Ferrari's startling Testarossa was everyone's fantasy about what a Super Ferrari should look like. It would sound menacing, it would be extremely fast, it would be painted blood red, and it would have the sort of style that made grown men weak at the knees.

Ferrari, in fact, evolved this car from the equally-famous Boxer, though they gave new four-valve heads to the 5-liter flat-12 engine, and commissioned this extraordinary style from Pininfarina. The strakes along the side led cooling air into the engine bay, and all Testarossas came with the same closed-roof shape.

Originally with 390bhp and with a 190mph top speed, this car was outstanding enough,

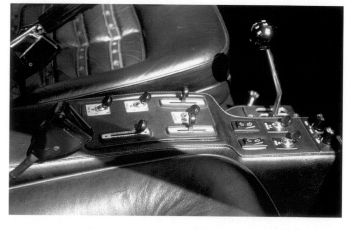

Above: Typical Ferrari style, even in the badge on a filler cap.

Top right: The dials' high figures revealed Ferrari's intent with this car.

Right: Stylish gear lever, and many other auxiliary controls.

Left: The horizontal styling motif of the Testarossa made the rear end look even wider than it actually was.

Below: The dramatic strakes channeled cooling air into the engine bay, on both sides of the car.

SPECIFICATIONS

Engine	4,942cc/301.8cu.in
Horsepower	390@6,300rpm
Top speed	171mph (275kph)
Wheelbase	98.5in (250.0cm)
Weight	3,675lb (1,667kg)
Sales	Not revealed

but as the years passed Ferrari made it better, and faster. The 428bhp 512TR, complete with a new nose, took over in 1992, and the 512M (modified yet again), took over in 1994 with 440bhp. With 0–100mph acceleration in just 10 seconds, this amazing car was nearly as fast as any mortal could envisage.

Above: The Ferrari Testarossa was a very well-packaged two-seater.

Far right: Hidden headlamps and a wide and flat nose were hallmarks.

Right: The engine bay of this car was an impressive sight.

Left: Although the Testarossa looked exciting at rest, it was even more exciting to drive. The sound and sensation of that massive engine, immediately behind the driver's ear, gave the most amazing adrenaline rush.

Right: Those who know say that the Testarossa could be tricky to drive at the limit, but for ordinary mortals it was an amazingly fast car to use safely on the road. Visibility from that low, but wide, cabin, was excellent.

FERRARI F40

In 1988 it was almost everyone's favorite new supercar, and it has kept that reputation ever since. Conceived as a fortieth birthday celebration of Ferrari, the F40 was, quite simply, the ultimate in road cars.

Mid-engined, of course, with a tubular chassis, of course, the F40 was all about function, performance, and delivery, for there were few concessions to comfort. The cabin looked as if it was that of a racing sports car and the turbocharged vee-8 engine definitely had a racing feel.

Ferrari had already developed the four-cam vee-8 theme for more than a decade before it started on the F40, but this was the most powerful yet. It produced a massive 478bhp from only 2.9-liters.

Ferrari's fortieth birthday present to itself was the 200mph F40.

SPECIFICATIONS

Engine	2,936cc/179cu.in
Horsepower	478@7,000rpm
Top speed	205mph (330kph)
Wheelbase	96.5in (245.0cm)
Weight	2,425lb (1,100kg)
Sales	1,200

Right: The F40 looked like a race car from every angle. That huge rear spoiler was meant to produce downforce at high road speeds.

Left: The 478bhp turbocharged 90-degree vee-8 engine of the F40 was mounted behind the cabin.

Right: Lots of wind-tunnel work resulted in a big rear spoiler, the vents along the side, and the twin NACA-style ducts in the main front panel.

Right: One interesting piece of F40 air-flow management was the use of tall, slim, air outlets behind the front wheels, to channel hot air out from the brakes.

Left: Like all the best competition-bred road cars, the Ferrari F40 was also an extremely practical machine. Access to all the running gear was by vast, lift-up, panels.

Below: Although the F40 was a road car, its interior was kitted out so that a proud owner could fully indulge himself on a racing circuit.

Above: Anyone who found a single line, contour, or fitting on the Ferrari F40 which was not exactly right for its job, was clearly not suited to one of the world's most exciting cars.

Right: Wide, flat, purposeful, ultra-fast and incredibly glamorous, the Ferrari F40 was the ultimate supercar two-seater of its day. It remains one of the greatest ever.

Left: With an F40 to drive, the open road ahead, on a great day, there could be little missing from a perfect motoring experience.

Left: The Ferrari 288GTO was the ultimate expression of the 308/328 theme, with a similar style. The big difference, though, was under the skin, where the 400bhp turbocharged vee-8 engine lay in a longitudinal position.

Below: The 288 GTO's vee-8 engine was longitudinally mounted behind the cabin, fitted with twin turbochargers, and developed a reliable 400bhp. The engine bay was absolutely stuffed full of machinery.

Above: From this view, although the family resemblance to the long-running 308/328 family is obvious, the extra wide stance of the rear wheels, and the GTO badge, tell us that this is the Ferrari 288GTO.

Right: This Ferrari 308/328-style Spider is a reminder that Pininfarina-shaped bodies could be not only beautiful, but practical too. The front corner of this car is a study in neat, purposeful design, with every detail catered for.

Left: The Ford RS200 was a rally car special, of which 200 were built in 1985/1986. All had mid-mounted, turbocharged engines and four-wheel-drive, plus this delicious Ghia-styled body. Standard road cars produced 250bhp from 1.8-liters, but the most powerful rallycross monsters had 650bhp/2.1-liter versions instead.

Right: When the GRP rear body section of the RS200 was lifted, the layout of the turbocharged engine, and its twinned spring/damper units, became clear.

Left: Lamborghini's Jalpa was a development of the Urraco of the 1970s. 410 such cars were sold in the 1980s.

Above: This was the well-equipped, but essentially simple, layout of the instrument display of the Lamborghini Jalpa.

Right: If the weather was right, what could be better than to drive around in this Lamborghini Jalpa with the roof panel removed?

Below: Early in the 1980s, Lancia produced the new Rally 037 model, a much more specialized derivative of the Beta Monte Carlo (or Scorpion, as it was always known in the USA). The Rally 037 had an in-line supercharged 2-liter engine behind the seats.

Far right top: Venturi was the model name of the French MVS Model, a brave attempt to take on both Renault (with its GTA) and, of course, Porsche.

Right: The MVS Venturi was a French-developed supercar which used a Renault vee-6 engine of 200bhp/2.5-liters. Neatly styled, with a body of fiberglass, it only sold slowly, but with a top speed of 155mph it was a real contender.

Far right bottom: The neat "MVS" logo tells all that is needed—for this was the small French company which produced the neat, Renault-powered, coupe in the 1980s.

Left: Venturi—not a commonly-known name, especially outside France, this MVS model was a nicely-engineered coupe which never built up the supercar reputation that it might have deserved.

Right: Clearly the MVS Venturi stylist took a long look at current shapes when preparing this new French shape in the mid-1980s, for there are cues and contours which had surely been seen, already, in cars like the Lotus Esprit, and the Renault Alpine GTA.

Left: The MVS Venturi was a pretty, if not quite outstanding shape, launched in a decade when most of the big manufacturers also had new styles to sell.

PORSCHE 959

Several manufacturers built new cars to meet the new Group B motorsport category, but the Porsche 959 was by far the finest example. Not only was it a stunningly capable 450bhp four-wheel-drive projectile, but it was civilized, carefully-developed, and built to Porsche's usual high standards.

Although based on the well-known 911, the 959 had new running gear with sophisticated four-wheel-drive, the turbocharged engine was an evolution of the world-famous 956 racing sports car power unit, and the style was altered to provide better aerodynamic performance.

Not only was this car extraordinarily fast—the top speed was nearly 200mph—but with

Top right: From this angle the 959's cabin looks just like that of any other 911-based car.

Right: The 959 power unit had twin turbochargers, twin intercoolers, and lots of control gear.

SPECIFICATIONS

Engine	2,851cc/154.0cu.in
Horsepower	450@6,500rpm
Top speed	197mph (317kph
Wheelbase	89.4in (227.2cm)
Weight	3,197lb (1,450kg)
Sales	250

The basis of the four-wheel-drive 959 was a 911 structure, but the front end had been carefully restyled.

Classic Profile

Below: The 959's style and structure was a modified version of the 911.

Far right: The 959 looked wickedly attractive from all angles.

Right: The 959 interior was similar to that of many 911s.

sophisticated four-wheel-drive its grip and traction were quite phenomenal, and the handling was as well-balanced as any supercar owner could wish. Except in the cost of running, it was every enthusiast's dream machine.

When new in 1987 it immediately became everyone's favorite Porsche, and all 250 of this strictly limited edition were speedily sold.

Right: To replace the long-running 308/328 family, Ferrari introduced the 348tb and ts (coupe and spider) models in 1989. Fitted with in-line versions of the famous vee-8 engines, these 300bhp/3.4-liter cars moved a step closer to being ultra-fast, ultra-civilized, road cars than earlier Ferraris had ever been.

Left: TVR's 420SEAC of 1986–1989 was almost the final evolution of the long-running Tasmin family. Its tubular chassis, and GRP Body hid a 300bhp Rover vee-8 engine, and its top speed was more than 150mph.

Left: Under the heavily slatted engine bay cover of the 348 there was a 300bhp/3.4-liter vee-8 engine.

Top right: Rear end badging included this discreet little badge on the engine lid itself.

Above: The nose of the 348 bore a clear family resemblance to the Ferrari Testarossa.

Right: The rear view mirrors of the 348ts were a pleasing, and wind-cheating, detail.

CHAPTER 5

1990s

The supercar excesses of the 1980s continued strongly into the 1990s, with new models from new manufacturers, and with 200mph now the minimum requirement for a credible all-new model. Not even a worldwide recession could kill off the supercar, though some found it difficult to find enough customers. But with McLaren's F1 reaching 230mph, had performance limits now been reached ?

The Dodge Viper of 1992 was a sensational spiritual successor to the Cobra, as its name confirms. Dodge used a new all-independent suspension chassis and a GRP body to hide a monstrous 400bhp vee-10 power unit.

Left: AC's Superblower model, complete with 355bhp/5.0-liter Ford-USA engine, was really the Cobra re-born. The style was not changed, though the engine was a new-generation vee-8.

Right: Ford rescued Aston Martin in the 1980s and soon developed this new model, the DB7, which transformed the company's fortunes. Much of the chassis, and the supercharged six-cylinder engine, were derived from Jaguar, but the beautiful style was unique. So was the performance—157mph.

Left: Bentley's Continental R was one the largest, most ponderous, but definite supercars of all time. Launched in 1991, it was a 385bhp machine which offered 150mph-plus.

Right: Although only a two-door car, the Bentley Continental R was a full four-seater—and beautifully trimmed.

Below: The Continental R was based on the platform of other Bentley/Rolls-Royce saloons of the period.

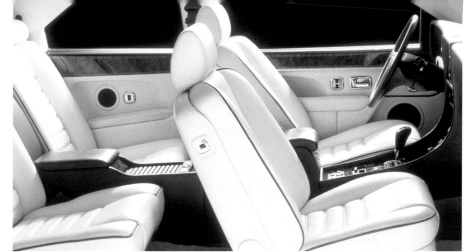

Left: The Continental R's chassis was amazingly poised for such a large car.

Right: The cabin of the Cizeta Moroder—function and equipment before space and style.

Below: On sale in 1992, the Cizeta Moroder V16T was the world's only vee-16 engined road car.

Left: Ferrari's new 456GT of 1992 was the company's first new front-engined car for two decades. With a 2+2 cabin and a 442bhp/5.5-liter vee-12, it was a 193mph machine.

Far left: Yet another superb Pininfarina style, on yet another superb Ferrari chassis, this being the 456GT of 1992.

Below: Although the 456GT looked like a sleek coupe, it was almost a four-seater, had a very civilized character, and was really the replacement for the long-running 400/412 saloons of the 1970s and 1980s.

ASTON MARTIN DB7 VANTAGE

Conceived in the 1990s and ready for sale as the century turned, the Aston Martin DB7 Vantage was a huge step forward for the Ford-owned concern. With competent all-independently suspended chassis, and a beautiful home-brewed body style, it was powered by a magnificent 420bhp/6.0-liter vee-12 engine. Ford-USA had conceived it, Cosworth had

Right: The complex instrument binnacle of the Aston Martin DB7 Vantage.

Right: The facia/instrument panel of the vee-12 engined Aston Martin DB7 Vantage.

finalized it and would build it, the result being the most powerful road car engine ever fitted by this company.

The Vantage was meant to be the ultimate in 2+2 road car transport—ultra-refined, well-equipped, and air-conditioned.

SPECIFICATIONS

Engine	5,935cc/362.3cu.in
Horsepower	420@6,000rpm
Top speed	185mph (298kph)
Wheelbase	102.0in (259.0cm)
Weight	3,575lb (1,621kg)
Sales	Not revealed

Strikingly similar to the Vanquish which followed, the DB7 Vantage was a compact 2+2 seater with sleek body lines, a 6-liter engine, and a 185mph top speed.

Left: To cool the 420bhp vee-12 engine of the DB7 Vantage, a large extra intake was needed under the nose.

Right: Ferrari upgraded the Testarossa in 1992, turning it into the 512TR, complete with 428bhp, and this new nose style.

Below: Jaguar's XJ220 was launched in 1989, and went on sale in 1992. Power was by a 542bhp twin-turbo, 3.5-liter, vee-6 engine which Jaguar had already raced.

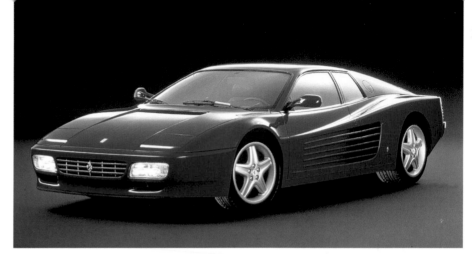

Above: Although it was large, the mid/rear-engined XJ220 was only a two-seater. Manufactured at a special factory, it was a superbly developed road car, which could reach 213mph.

Left: The XJ220 had a wide expanse of dials, controls, and switches. Lower than most other supercars, it was nevertheless very comfortable and civilized to drive.

Right: The XJ220's fine lines hide the fact that it was one of the widest production cars ever put on sale. Although there were no spoilers, this was an extremely stable platform at high speeds.

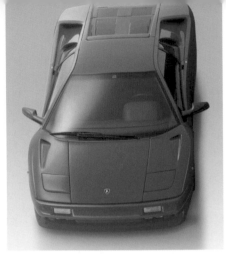

Left: The Lamborghini Diablo was a straight replacement for the popular Countach, and went on sale in 1990.

Far left: Like its predecessor, the Diablo had a powerful (492bhp) 5.7liter vee-12 engine behind the cabin.

Right: Lamborghini's Diablo had a super-voluptuous body style.

Below: Marcello Gandini's style for the Diablo featured a constantly rising theme along the flanks. This truly was a "cab-forward" layout.

BUGATTI EB110

The Italian entrepreneur Romano Artioli bought up the rights to the long-dead Bugatti name, and revived it in 1991, as a born-again Italian supercar. The result was the EB110, a brutally-efficient 550bhp monster which delivered its promise on the road, but failed in an unfavorable recession-hit market place.

Like all the best current supercars, it featured a mid/rear engine position, with power by a 3.5-liter vee-12 which had four tiny turbochargers. This was linked to four-wheel-drive, and since it was developed and built in Modena (close to Ferrari, Maserati, and Lamborghini), it was expected to be a competent 212mph performer.

Although the EB110 was a great car, it was ultra-expensive, even in this heady market. This, and long delays in starting up series production, killed it off early.

With no less than 550bhp to keep in check, Bugatti needed plentiful air flow through the engine bay. The rear spoiler was there to trim the handling.

SPECIFICATIONS

Engine	3,500cc/213.6cu.in
Horsepower	550@8,000
Top speed	212mph (341kph)
Wheelbase	100.4in (255.0cm)
Weight	3,571lb (1620kg)
Sales	Less than 20

The Bugatti EB110 style preserved a pastiche of the famous old Bugatti "horseshoe" grille, but the rest of the nose was given up to air intakes and rectangular headlamps.

Left: Maserati's image was reborn in the late 1990s with this smart, front vee-8 engined, 3200GT model. By this time, Ferrari had taken over the concern.

Right: Giugiaro styled the new range of Maseratis. The nose of the 3200GT was rounded, efficient, and carefully detailed, to include the famous trident badge.

Below: Giugiaro's style for the Maserati 3200GT included a carefully rounded and integrated tail, complete with integral transverse spoiler.

Left: The Mercedes-Benz CLK-GTR was an amazing limited-production coupe, meant to go racing, but built in tiny numbers to meet the regulations.

Bottom left: The CLK-GTR was not very practical for road use, if only because ground clearance was minimal. The color scheme was specified by the buyer.

Below: In theory there were connections between the CLK-GTR and the CLK road car, but apart from the front grille, no-one ever found out what they were.

Above: The engine bay of the CLK-GTR was exposed under an expanse of plexiglass, and that aerofoil was very functional.

Top right: How do you fancy driving a CLK-GTR in a traffic jam? Not at all, maybe— but it would be great as an autobahn express.

Right: The CLK-GTR was powered by a 612bhp/6.9-liter version of the Mercedes-Benz vee-12 road-car engine.

Left: TVR's Chimaera convertible was available with 288bhp/4.5-liter, or 326bhp/5.0-liter Rover-based vee-8 engines, and could reach 165mph.

Below: The Chimaera's two-seater cabin was very compact, and had this quirky facia/instrument display.

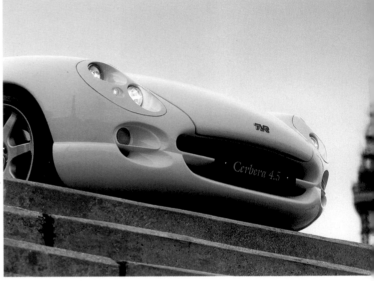

Left: Introduced in 1993, the TVR Chimaera was a front-vee-8-engined coupe featuring a rather cramped 2+2 cabin. The own-brand 420bhp/4.5-liter engine provided up to 200mph.

Above: TVR was proud of its Blackpool, England connections, which explains the presence of the famous Tower in this study of the Cerbera's distinctive nose.

Right: In 1995 the 2+2 Cerbera was the largest and longest TVR sports car so far launched. With a style developed entirely by the tiny British company, it was an impressive performer.

DODGE VIPER

In 1992 the launch of the Dodge Viper was encouraged by Chrysler's enthusiastic President, Bob Lutz. Looking to repeat the success of the AC Cobra of the 1960s, he commissioned this rip-roaring all-American roadster. With its simple tubular chassis, and a voluptuous GRP body shell, Viper power was by a 400bhp/8.0-liter vee-10 engine which had been heavily-modified from a Chrysler truck unit.

North America had never built such cars before (the Cobra had been an Anglo-US hybrid), so Lutz knew it had to be outstanding. With so much

SPECIFICATIONS

Engine	7,997cc/488.0cu.in
Horsepower	400@4,600rpm
Top speed	160mph (257.4kph)
Wheelbase	96.2in (244.3cm)
Weight	3,200lb (1,452kg)
Sales	14,680 (1992–2002)

Far right: The Dodge Viper's venomous looks matched its name.

Right: Neat headlamp pods and a truly aggressive grille.

power, with a bellowing exhaust note, and with such extrovert character, there was no danger of it ever being ignored. It was exactly the supercar that Americans all wanted, and in the first ten years nearly 15,000 were sold.

Left: This Viper GTS-R derivative won many endurance races.

Below: The Viper II facia/instrument display had an impressive layout.

Right: The Viper II offered 500bhp power and an exhilarating drive.

Left: Some cars are pretty, but some are aggressively attractive—the Viper was certainly one of the latter. No-one could ignore its character.

Below: When shaping the Viper, Chrysler's stylists clearly studied everything which had attracted Americans to customized Cobras.

Left: After development throughout the 1990s, in 2002 Aston Martin revealed the Zagato-styled derivative of the DB7 Vantage, a short-wheelbase 450bhp two-seater.

Right: The famous Italian name of "Zagato" had been linked with Aston Martin on previous occasions.

Right: Zagato's treatment of the DB7 Vantage was typically "up front," with a massive grille dominating the nose.

Below: Once VW had taken over at Bentley, it commissioned this imposing mid-engined project car, the Hunaudières.

Right: Not only did the Hunaudières project car have four-wheel-drive, but a 623bhp/8.0-liter W16 engine, which would guarantee a top speed of more than 200mph.

Left: The Ferrari F355 arrived in 1994, and immediately gained the title of the "best ever Ferrari." Mid-engined, with 380bhp/3.5-liter, vee-8 power, it was beautiful, well-balanced, and handled like a current race car.

Below: The F355's engine was the latest evolution of the long-running Ferrari vee-8, now with five valves per cylinder.

Above: Ferrari F355's carrying the "F1" logo meant that they were fitted with the latest "paddle shift" gearchange, with levers behind the steering wheel.

Right: The F355's engine produced 380bhp—or 108.5bhp/liter—a phenomenal output for a normally-aspirated power unit from any manufacturer.

Far right: With the F355 style, Pininfarina somehow excelled all its previous standards, for this was a wonderfully balanced, and superfast, car.

FERRARI F550 MARANELLO

Breaking with every tradition, Ferrari announced this front-engined two-seater, the F550 Maranello, in 1996, as a replacement for the long-running mid-engined Testarossa family. Carrying more than a touch of the legendary Daytona DNA in its genes, this was a modern sports Ferrari for a modern era.

Right: Ferrari's "Prancing Horse" was proudly displayed on the tail of the 550 Maranello, one of the sleekest supercars ever to come from the Italian concern.

The 550 Maranello was laid out as a spacious two-seater coupe.

SPECIFICATIONS

Engine	5,474cc/334.0cu.in
Horsepower	479@7,000
Top speed	199mph (320kph)
Wheelbase	98.4in (250.0cm)
Weight	3,733lb (1,693kg)
Sales	Introduced in 1996

Left: Four huge exhaust outlets, two at each side—well, what else would you expect...?

Below: The 550 Maranello's front style included a large air scoop in the hood, which fed fresh air directly to the air-cleaners of the 5.5-liter vee-12 engine.

Naturally there was a resemblance to the larger 456GT, especially in the vee-12 engine, but this was otherwise a near-unique "take" on the supercar theme. The latest chassis layout was made out of aluminum, and naturally the body shell was mainly paneled in the same material.

With so much power, a six-speed manual gearbox, and a slippery shape, a near-200mph performance was guaranteed, all in peace, quiet, and with the unique Ferrari aura.

Left: Jaguar introduced the new front-engined XK8 range of coupes and convertibles in 1996. All of them had a brand-new 4.0-liter vee-8 engine.

Far left: As a replacement for the XJS, the XK8 could not have looked more different. The most powerful of all, the XKR, had a 370bhp super-charged version of the vee-8 engine.

Below: It is difficult to make coupe and convertible versions of any car look absolutely right, but Jaguar achieved this with the XK8.

Left: When Jaguar's XK was fitted with the 370bhp supercharged engine, it was badged XKR—the most potent.

Below: The Jaguar XKR's smooth vee-8 engine revved smoothly up to nearly 7,000rpm and could reach 155mph.

Right: Advertising? For the XKR, Jaguar added the discreet wording "Supercharged" to the famous hood badge.

HONDA NSX

Although Honda started building cars in the 1960s, the Japanese company did not produce a true supercar, the NSX, until 1990. It was as advanced, as capable, and as thoughtfully detailed as expected.

Because Honda chose to use a transversely-mounted mid-engined layout, the style of its first supercar was quite conventional. Like similar Ferraris of this period, the NSX had a low nose, and the engine (a four-cam vee-6 in this case), was transversely-mounted behind the cabin. The car was developed at a time when Honda was heavily involved in F1 motor racing, and the driver Ayrton Senna was involved in the testing.

The Honda NSX was the first-ever Japanese supercar, and was fitted with a 274bhp/3.0-liter V6 engine behind the seats.

Above: Cooling air for the mid-mounted engine had to be channeled in by way of scoops in the flanks.

Right: Take away the badge, and one might so easily have been looking at a Ferrari...

SPECIFICATIONS

Engine	2,977cc/181.7cu.in
Horsepower	274@7,000
Top speed	167mph (268.7kph)
Wheelbase	99.6in (253.0cm)
Weight	3,020lb (1,370kg)
Sales	Introduced in 1990

Below: Some of the NSX's facia and instrument features had already been seen on other models from this popular marque.

Far right: Although the NSX had a tightly-profiled body structure, every effort was made to make all parts serviceable.

Right: The NSX's vee-6 engine was a power-tuned evolution of the unit already found in the Honda Legend.

The major advance came in the monocoque structure, which was almost entirely crafted from aluminum. Not only did this make the whole car lighter, but more fuel efficient, and somehow easier to drive.

Although this was a capable car in so many ways, it took time to build a reputation and, ten years on, was mechanically improved without many changes to the looks.

Left: Porsche introduced its new limited-production 911 GT3 in 1999. With a 360bhp version of the water-cooled 3.6-liter flat-six engine, it could rush up to 187mph.

Below: The 911 GT3 of 1999 was based on normal 911s, with new and aerodynamically purposeful front and rear spoilers, and with extended sills under the doors.

Above: The 911 GT3 was a pure two-seater where performance, function, and driving comfort came first.

Right: The last of the classic air-cooled 911s (known by the factory as the "993" type) were built in the late 1990s.

Left: Porsche introduced the 911 GT3 to convince the clientele that the 911 had not "gone soft." It was very, very fast...

McLAREN F1

Until any other car maker produces a car which can beat 230mph, McLaren's F1 three-seater will always be the world's fastest car. Designed from the outset to be the ultimate road car, the F1 had a composite tub, a three-seater layout with the driver's seat in the center of the car, and a purpose-built 6.1-liter BMW vee-12 engine behind the seats.

In every way it was a no-compromise design. It also cost an alarming amount of money— $800,000 in 1993, when it went on sale. Sales were slow, but its reputation was high.

SPECIFICATIONS

Engine	6,064cc/370 cu.in
Horsepower	627@7,400rpm
Top speed	231mph (371.6kph)
Wheelbase	107.0in (271.8cm)
Weight	2,509lb (1,138kg)
Sales	100

Far right: The McLaren F1 was a large and long car, but not an inch was wasted.

Right: This was the first supercar to have a three-seater cabin.

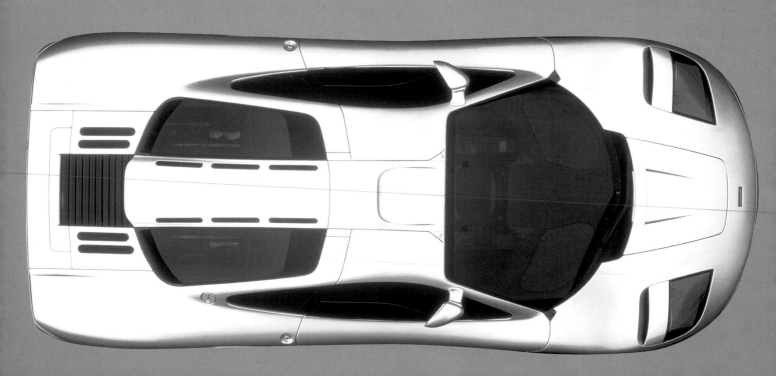

McLaren F1
engineering was
by ex-Brabham F1
designer Gordon
Murray, while the
styling was by Peter
Stevens, who had
already done great
work for Lotus.

Below: TVR's Chimaera was a relatively simply-engineered supercar, with a multi-tube chassis, a GRP body style, and a choice of front-mounted Rover-based vee-8 engines.

Right: TVR believed in keeping their cars simple, so in the Chimaera there was no semi-automatic option, no high-tech dials, and no superfluity of control gear.

Left: Although the TVR Chimaera was only a two-seater, it was quite a large vehicle. It also had sizeable stowage space—a rare feature in a supercar.

Above: To replace the F40, Ferrari spent years developing a new top-line two-seater—the F50.

Right: The 4.7-liter, vee-12 engine of the F50 was a productionized version of the 1990 Ferrari F1 power unit.

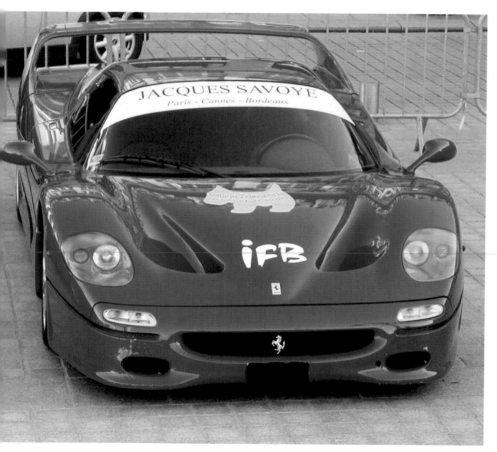

Above: Although the nose of the F50 looks none too smooth, a lot of thought had gone into getting the right airflow into the radiators.

Far left: The dramatic rear view of the Ferrari F50 shows a high transverse rear spoiler, which was really a re-statement of the F40 theme.

Left: Further decorated with a French Ferrari dealer's logos, this F50 was one of only 349 such 202mph supercars made.

Left: The styling of the TVR Griffith of 1992 was so right that it needed absolutely no decoration.

Below: The Griffith's rear quarter was smoothly detailed, with no separate rear fender.

Right: The front plate pictured here denotes the final specification of the 325bhp/5.0-liter engined model.

Below: The cabin of the TVR Griffith shows the facia instrument display: interestingly enough, for a car built in the late 1990s, there was no airbag in the steering wheel.

Right: Only the minimum of airflow management testing showed that this elegant arrangement was the way to get warm air away from the front-mounted cooling radiator.

CHAPTER

2000s

As the new century opened, the supercar was better and faster than ever before. Not only did established manufacturers such as Ferrari continue to produce new models, but new marques entered the fray, like Saleen from the US, Pagani from Italy and Koenigsegg from Denmark, Bugatti and Bentley, both returning their image for the new era.

And the new Swedish Koenigsegg CC8S was different, it looked like a conventional supercar, but it had one unique feature—it was Swedish

Left: Although VW completely changed the type of car that Bentley would be building in the new century, they preserved the legendary badge, the "winged B."

Far left: There was no comparison between this VW-sponsored Bentley Continental GT, and any previous model to carry that name.

Below: With a front-mounted W12 power unit, the "engine room" of the new Bentley Continental GT could be small. The result was that this became a compact four-seater supercar.

Left: Bentley testing in the snows of Sweden showed just how effective the four-wheel-drive chassis could be. Will all future supercars be like this?

Below: High-tech. with tradition in the Bentley—a six-speed ZF automatic transmission surrounded by acres of top-quality wood and leather.

ASTON MARTIN VANQUISH

Launched in 2001, the Aston Martin Vanquish
was the first of the new generation of cars from
this Ford-owned company. Powered by the
fabulous Cosworth-built 6.0-liter vee-12
engine, it featured an aluminum structure, and
this stunning two-door 2+2 body style.

Technical features included a six-
speed transmission (as used
in the Dodge Viper),
with

SPECIFICATIONS

Engine	5,925cc/361.7cu.in
Horsepower	460@6,500rpm
Top speed	196mph (315kph)
Wheelbase	105.9in (269.0cm)
Weight	4,046lb (1,835kg)
Sales	Introduced in 2001

Left: The speedometer of the Vanquish read up to 210mph. In suitable conditions the car could almost reach the limit of that calibration.

Below: The Vanquish's facia/instrument layout put function ahead of beauty. The center panel was incredibly technical-looking.

Right: Because aerodynamic performance is now so important, modern supercars like the Aston Martin Vanquish have no separate fenders to give crash protection.

paddle-shift controls behind the steering wheel, many aluminum components in the all-independent suspension installation, and an engine that was electronically limited to 7,200rpm.

Like the ancient vee-8 engined Virage generation that it replaced, the new Vanquish was set for a long life, and its 460bhp power output was only the start of things to come. With 200mph performance, who cared that fuel economy was down at about 13mpg?

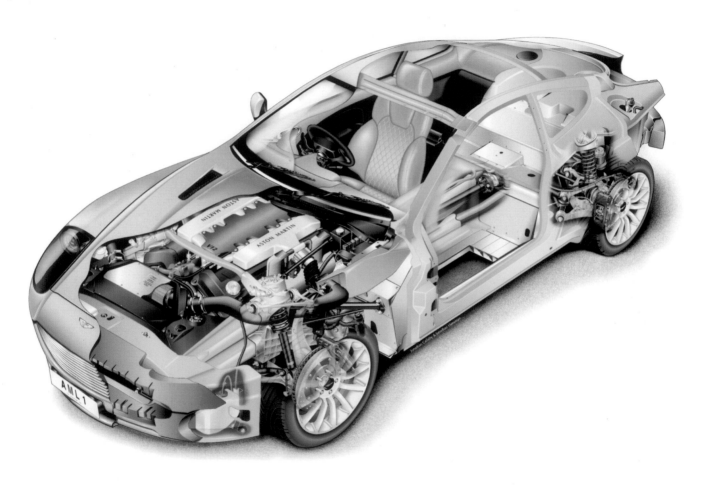

Left: This stunning "ghosted" drawing of the Aston Martin Vanquish shows an engine bay crammed with machinery, and detail of the all-independent suspension chassis.

Below: Good-versus-Evil in a recent "James Bond" film, with our hero driving an Aston Martin Vanquish, ahead of the villain in his Jaguar XKR.

Left: Cadillac don't only make limousines... The badge on the nose of the Cien project car proved that they could also build a supercar.

Far left: BMW's Z8 Roadster brought brute power back into the BMW range, and also provided just a hint of 507 style from the 1950s.

Below: The Cadillac Cien was only a one-off, but it showed that North American engineers could match the Europeans at their own supercar game.

Below: Hidden away behind the fat wheelarches and the spoiler of the Cadillac Cien was a specially-developed 750bhp/7.5-liter vee-12 engine.

Far right: Every sharply-profiled line of the Cadillac Cien project supercar had a purpose—in this case to channel air into the front cooling radiator package.

Right: Detailing of a modern supercar is always enthralling to study. A look along the flanks of the Cadillac Cien shows up its delicately changing profile.

Above: The Dodge Viper had real performance, as this kph speedometer (the Imperial equivalent was a 220mph instrument!) proves.

Top right: Look closely, but don't touch! The highly stylized Dodge Viper badge.

Left: In 2002 the second-generation Viper arrived, to build on the great success of the original. The basic front-engined vee-10 layout was not changed, but the lines were subtly smoother.

Right: Low-mounted extra driving lamps, the corner of the front grille and the row of headlamps—all Viper details, and all part of the distinctive, serpentine look to match the name.

Left: Do you remember when headlamps were large, circular, and out in the breeze? Not any more, not on the Dodge Viper.

Below: The closed fastback GTS-R version of the original-shape Viper was meant to go motor racing, and to win. It did —many times, on several continents.

Right: Ten years after the first Viper hit the streets, Dodge showed the second-generation model, whose frontal-lines had been sharpened up, and whose flanks told a different story.

FERRARI F360 MODENA

How many suggested that Ferrari could never improve on the sensational F355 of the 1990s? They were all wrong, because the F360 Modena was faster, even smoother in its style, better engineered, and another logical step forward.

The F360 was the first of a whole new generation of Ferrari supercars, in that it had an all-aluminum structure, with an aluminum body shell, but its theme was as before. Here was a compact two-seater, with a magnificent 400bhp engine, and a top speed of 185mph, looking as every Pininfarina-shaped coupe should, and positively exuding class.

Unless one needed more cabin space, why bother even looking at a larger supercar of any make?

Left: The Pininfarina-styled F360 Modena shared many styling cues with other models.

Right: Ferrari styles got progressively smoother with every new model, the F360 included.

SPECIFICATIONS

Engine	3,586cc/219.0cu.in
Horsepower	400@8,500rpm
Top speed	184mph (296.0kph)
Wheelbase	102.3in (260.0cm)
Weight	3,191lb (1,447kg)
Sales	Introduced in 1999

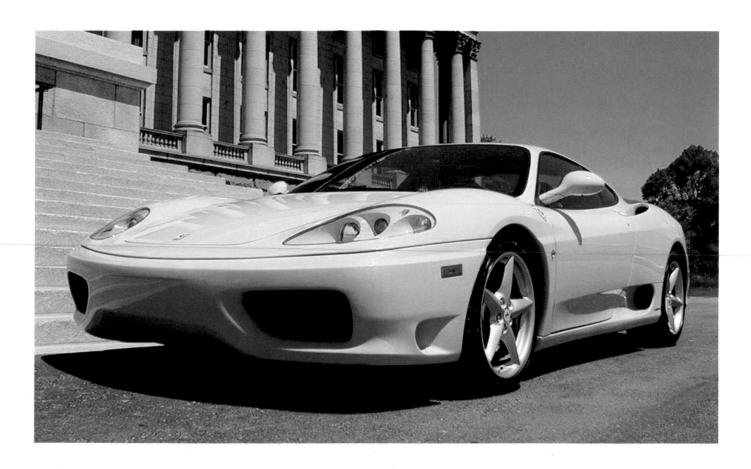

Below: As the new century opened, the Ferrari 575M took over from the 550 Maranello, looking the same as before, but with an enlarged, 515bhp, vee-12 engine.

Right: Nearly forty years after the original was designed, Ford decided to re-create the GT40, this time making it larger, and calling it the Ford GT. Sales began in 2003.

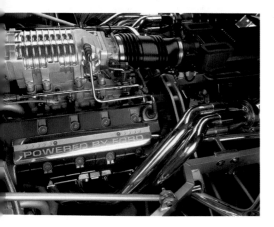

Above: An engine bay full of supercharged vee-8 engine in the new-generation Ford GT. No lack of performance, sound, or character here.

Left: 1960s style Ford GT40, or 2003 GT? Difficult to spot unless you are a Ford fanatic.

Right: Simple though well-equipped, with figure hugging seats and full-harness safety belts, this was the driving seat of the 2003 Ford GT.

Left: In 1994 Christian von Koenigsegg of Sweden set out with just one aim—to build the world's fastest road car. The result, unveiled in 2000, was the mid/rear-engined CC8S, claimed to be capable of 242mph.

Right: Most mid-engined Supercars have the same kind of cabin, but the Koenigsegg's is different. The driver has to control a 240mph machine.

Below: The Koenigsegg CC8S's supercharged Ford V8 engine sits behind the cabin.

Left: Christian von Koenigsegg made sure that his driver was placed well forward, towards the front of the car—that being one of the shortest supercar noses of all.

Right: Koenigsegg claims that the door opening mechanism on the CC8S is unique, describing it as a "dihedral synchro-helix actuation system."

Left: Maserati's 4200 Spyder, introduced in 2001, took the rebirth of the Italian company a stage further. With a 385bhp engine, it could reach 177mph.

Below: Two versions of Maserati's 4200 chassis were available—a closed coupe, and this shorter-wheelbase open-top Spyder. The front-end style was shared.

Above: The Maserati 4200 Spyder was a self-indulgent two-seater, now backed by Ferrari finance and expertise. It was front-engined, and like all the best Maseratis, it featured a torquey vee-8 engine.

Right: Coming from a tiny, new, company in England, the Noble M12 GTO looked the part. With a 310bhp, turbocharged Ford-USA vee-6 engine, it was a much lighter car than many of its rivals.

Left: The Noble M12GTO had a mid/rear-mounted, vee-6 engine, and a compact two-seater cabin.

Below: Was there a touch of Lotus in the style of the Noble M12 GTO? The Leicester-based concern angrily denies this, claiming its own artistic themes.

Right: Because the Ford-USA vee-6 was a compactly packaged engine, this allowed the Noble M12 GTO to be smaller and a lot lighter than some of its rivals. A 150mph-plus top speed was assured.

LAMBORGHINI MURCIELAGO

Lamborghini made several abortive attempts to replace the long-running Diablo before settling on this Murcielago model in 2001. From a company now securely controlled by Audi of Germany, this project re-thought the mid-rear engined layout in every detail, though one final evolution of the legendary vee-12 engine was retained.

Here was a mixture of tradition, and modern high-tech. Although the chassis was a multi-tube steel structure, and the engine well-known, the body was mainly built of carbon fiber, ABS brakes were standardized, and there was electronic adaptive control of suspension damper settings.

Amazingly, no spoilers or other aerodynamic aides were needed to add on to the smooth, in-house, style. With a top speed of 205mph, this family was obviously only at the beginning of its development life.

SPECIFICATIONS	
Engine	6,192cc/378.0cu.in
Horsepower	571@7,500rpm
Top speed	205mph (330.0kph)
Wheelbase	105.0in (266.5cm)
Weight	3,638lb (1,650kg)
Sales	Introduced in 2001

Right: The Murcielago's doors opened upwards, exactly as those of the Diablo had always done.

Below: The cabin of the Murcielago.

This was the rear end
of the new Lamborghini
Murcielago. Amazingly,
for a car which could
top 200mph, there were
no spoilers fitted to
add downforce.

Above: The Pagani Zonda C12 was all about function, not pure beauty, with a clear race-car heritage.

Left: The tail of the Pagani Zonda was unmistakable, with its protruding cluster of exhaust pipes.

Far left: Purposeful and functional, if not as beautiful as some rivals, the Zonda was an effective supercar.

Left: Zonda power came from an AMG-modified 7.3-liter, Mercedes-Benz vee-12, which produced a solid 555bhp at 5,900rpm.

Below: The Zonda's roof was so low, and the cabin so like a race car, that the steering wheel had to be re-shaped to allow space for the driver's legs.

Right: More of a civilized racing sports coupe than a general-purpose road car, the Pagani Zonda C12 had enormous rear tires, but a very narrow two-seater cabin.

MOSLER MT 900S

The Mosler MT900 was one of several North American supercar projects which came to fruition at the beginning of the new century.

Conceived by Rod Trenne, but financed by Warren Mosler, the MT900 was a mid/rear-engined car which could be sold in two guises

—one for GT racing, the other for road car use. MT900S meant "street car," while "R" denoted the race-car derived version of it.

Engineered like a race car, with an aluminum monocoque, the MT900 was powered by a modified Chevrolet Corvette vee-8 engine which had conventional overhead-valve operation, but had an aluminum block and cylinder heads. The coupe body style complied with GT race car regulations, and was made from carbon fiber panels and sections.

Although this was an expensive machine, it was also very practical, for much of the chassis engineering was based on Corvette components, and road cars had air-conditioning, ABS braking, traction control, and power assisted steering.

Left: The Mosler MT900S had a passenger cabin laid out with quiet good taste. Many components were derived from the Chevrolet Corvette sports car.

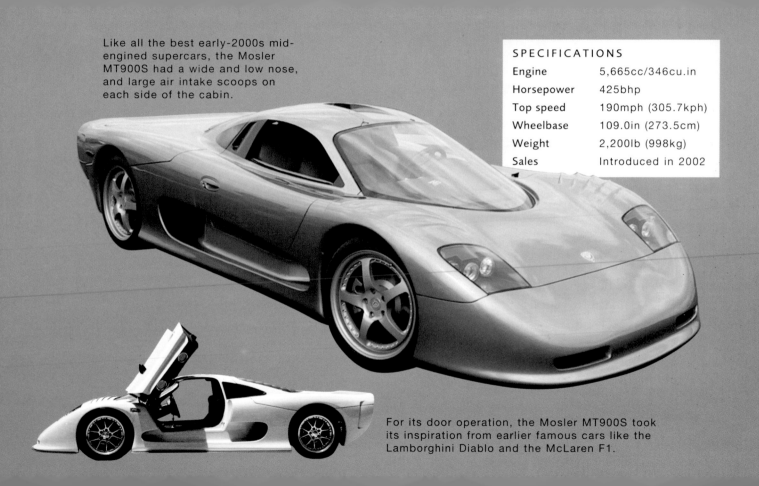

Like all the best early-2000s mid-engined supercars, the Mosler MT900S had a wide and low nose, and large air intake scoops on each side of the cabin.

SPECIFICATIONS

Engine	5,665cc/346cu.in
Horsepower	425bhp
Top speed	190mph (305.7kph)
Wheelbase	109.0in (273.5cm)
Weight	2,200lb (998kg)
Sales	Introduced in 2002

For its door operation, the Mosler MT900S took its inspiration from earlier famous cars like the Lamborghini Diablo and the McLaren F1.

Above: The Panoz Esperante's aluminum body hid a front-mounted Ford Mustang engine with 320bhp, along with the car's transmission, suspension, and brakes.

Left: The Panoz Esperante was an elegant, well-designed two-seater which was ideal for cruising open roads in warm, sunny climates.

Right: By comparison with many other supercars, the USA-inspired Panoz used many familiar Ford components, which helped limit costs. Nevertheless, this was a 155mph car.

Left: In 2001, Porsche's new 911 GT2 had a 462bhp turbocharged version of the water-cooled, flat-six engine. With a top speed of nearly 200mph, this was a phenomenal road and track car.

Right: Compared with the normal 911 Turbo, the 2001-model GT2 had a new front lower panel, extra scoops into the engine bay, and extended sills.

Below: The Porsche 911 GT2 had a big rear spoiler, not for decoration, but to trim the high-speed handling of this 462bhp machine.

Left: Porsche's 911GT2 of 2001 was a purposeful beast, with a 462bhp engine, which could reach nearly 200mph. Though developed primarily with racing in mind, it was a totally civilized road car. The styling was as distinctively 911 as ever...

Below: In 2002 Ferrari carried on the famous F40 and F50 line by introducing a car coded F60, but officially badged "Enzo." Maybe not the sleekest mid/rear-engined Ferrari ever launched, it was certainly an impressive 650bhp/217mph beast.

Below: The famous "Prancing Horse" badge was proudly mounted in several different locations on the Enzo.

Left: It was no coincidence that the nose of the 2002 Enzo supercar copied the front-wing profile of Ferrari's F1 single-seaters of the period. There was a cooling radiator immediately behind that air inlet.

Above: Massive carbon brakes, with huge Brembo calipers were hidden behind the five-spoke alloy wheels of Ferrari's latest Enzo model.

Right: Nice touch—tail, brake, and turn indicator lamps mounted in twinned circular housings at the rear of the Enzo.

Below: Maybe the rear of the Enzo did not look unified, or all-enveloping, but those scoops and air outlets were all needed to keep the 650bhp/6.0-liter vee-12 cool in all conditions.

Left: Like several other car-makers, Saleen looked to McLaren and Lamborghini for inspiration when laying out the door operation of its S7 model.

Overleaf: Powered by an overhead-valve, 7-liter Ford-USA vee-8 engine, the American Saleen S7 was a dream car with ground-effect bodywork, and a claimed top speed of at least 200mph.

Below: Styled in America, with American engineering throughout the chassis, the Saleen S7 was a big but very elegant mid/rear-engined supercar.

Index

PICTURE CREDITS

The majority of photographs in this book were taken by Nicky Wright,
but the author and publishers would also like to thank the many
automobile manufacturers who kindly supplied photographs
from their archives and contemporary photo galleries.